THE CODE AGENCY

A GRIMM MYSTERY

EAGLEBRITE

CONTENTS

ISBN: 978-1-7366454-3-7

Thekidcode.org

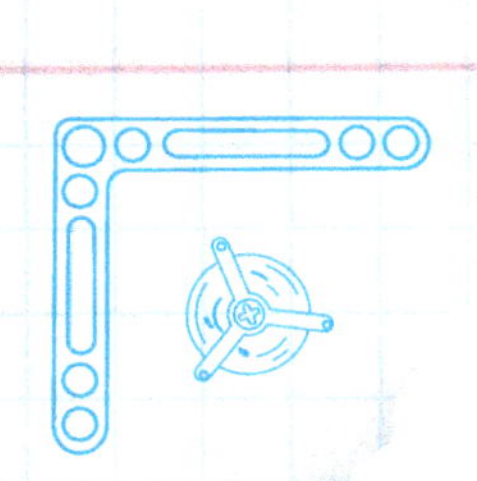

Parent Detective

If your child is inquisitive loves to ask "why" and puzzles are an adventure.. This can be a fun book for them!. The Code Agency is a book that takes your child on a journey to get them UNPLUGGED from the computer and video games but still learning about
Computer Science all while having fun and becoming a part of a crew of master puzzlers. Being in the Technology field for more than 15 years and working at places such as AT&T and Northwestern University have deepened my love for technology. I want to share this excitement for the next generation of tinkers, innovators and out of the box thinkers. I hope you and your family enjoy the journey.

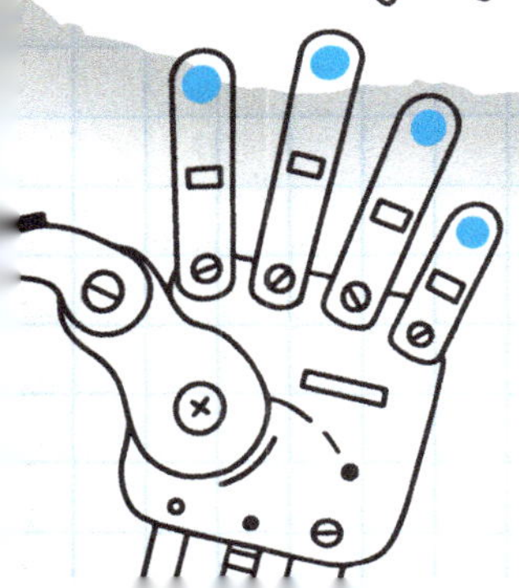

A journey starts in a place unseen and your heart can and will create beautiful things.

LAUREN R. GRIFFIN

WELCOME

TO

THE CODE AGENCY

What's The Code Agency?

I'm glad you asked, we're a few kids who love to solve puzzles and mysteries.

We're also Spy Detectives Agents (S.D Agents) but we'll talk about that later.

If you like puzzles and mysteries come on and join the crew.

The next few pages you are about to read are.....CLASSIFED. I'll introduce you to the crew.

RESTRICTED ACCESS

S.D AGENTS ONLY

CLASSIFIED PROFILES

CLASSIFIED

DEE E.

Likes: I like to investigate things to see how they work. I can break large things down into smaller chunks.

Strength: I like to think of myself as a leader, and I make good decisions. I'm honest and I care a lot about people. Problem solving is kind of my thing.

Dislikes: Big bulky and clunky stuff.

EXTRA's

Where I need to improve: I don't like when things are not neat or clear and straight forward. Sometimes I miss a few details, so I need to work on that.

When angry or upset: I like to be alone with my thoughts.

Fun Fact: I like to find secret entryways and hidden things.

"MAC ABSTRACT"

Likes: I like to find out "why" things work. I also love animals!

Strength: Finding the hidden stuff that make important things work. I don't leave a question unanswered.

Dislikes: Disorganization is a no for me. And I don't really like being alone, like Dee. It's just me and my mother at home, and she works a lot, so I'm often alone, and bored.

EXTRA's

Where I need to improve: I sometimes look too hard in the details.

When angry or upset: I can get really angry and lose my temper sometimes.

Fun Fact: I like riddles, so I sometimes speak in riddles.

"PATTY PATTERN"

Likes: I love patterns and everything that is artistic and creative. I also like to see how things work together.

Strength: I can see how each part works together so everything works in harmony with each other. I create different ways for things to fit together.

Dislikes: When the patterns don't come together.

EXTRA's

Where I need to improve: I sometimes get focused on the pattern and can make things that don't solve the problem.

When angry or upset: I get distracted, I lose my focus, drift off into a daydream. (That's when I do artwork, it helps to calm me).

Fun Fact: I like design a lot! I love doing artwork and creating art out of unusual objects and materials.

"AL AND ALLIE ALGORITHM"

Likes: We are twins who love solving riddles. We like to create instructions with computer code that helps people solve problems or tasks.

Strength: Computer coding of course! A host of other things, too many to list here.

Dislikes: When instructions are not clear. Yuck! We also don't like being compared to each other. We don't want computers to do everything just help with certain things.

EXTRA's

Where we need to improve: We can sometimes be too detailed, and the code ends up in a forever loop we can't stop.

When angry or upset: We often bicker but mostly in fun. Sometimes we get nasty though, and we really know how to argue with each other!

Fun Fact: Last year we hacked into the school's website for Mr. Field. And recently we made a robot that does all our chores for us!

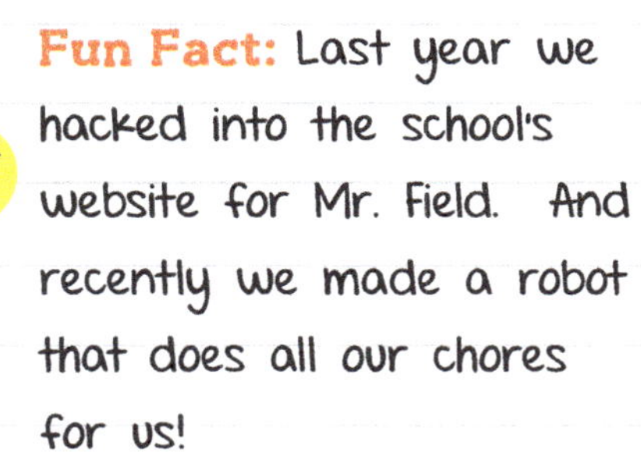

DETECTIVE TRAINING

Hi, it's Dee again! Now that you know everyone, in order to join The Code Agency there are a few brain buzzing puzzles you'll have to solve to become a Spy Detective Agent (S.D Agent).

Don't worry we know you're a genius and this will be a slice of cake for you.

Did someone say cake?

Mac you're always hungry! It's not real cake...

Anyway, back to what I was saying. Everyone in the crew had to go through the training and we know you'll do great.

We believe in you!

By the way..... When we solve our mysteries sometimes we create computer programs and inventions to help us..

Once you finish training we'll move on to solving more mysteries and inventing new things..

The puzzles in this book are a part of what we call The Detective Code. "The Detective Code" helps us to solve our mysteries too.

-- It's your choice. --

(A) If you want to know more about "The Detective Code" you can go to page 194

or

(B) Start Training! Go to page 24 and start the puzzles.

We created this Detective Code flash card for you.

DETECTIVE CODE IN A FLASH

* **EXAMINATION** - Focuses on the main part of the puzzle in order to solve it..
* **ABSTRACTION** - Remove any unnecessary pieces of information and focus on key important pieces to solve the puzzle.
* **PATTERNS** - The pattern in the puzzle might help to solve the puzzle.
* **ALGORITHMS** - Use a set of steps or instructions to solve the puzzle.

DRAW YOUR OWN S.D AGENT PROFILE

Draw an image of yourself

Fill in information for your S.D Agent profile

Likes:

Strength:

Dislikes:

Where I can improve:

When angry or upset:

Fun Fact:

EXAMINATION FUN

You Examine things everyday!

You use examination to make a peanut butter and jelly sandwich or any one of your favorite sandwich's. You have to figure our what goes on the sandwich then get the ingredients but if you didn't know what went on the sandwich you wouldn't know what to get.

Examination puzzles!

The next few puzzles you will need to examine and focus on different parts of the puzzle in order to solve it.

Sketch Code - 1

"X" marks the spy - Pattern Code

Use the Blank Code blocks to copy the above pattern.

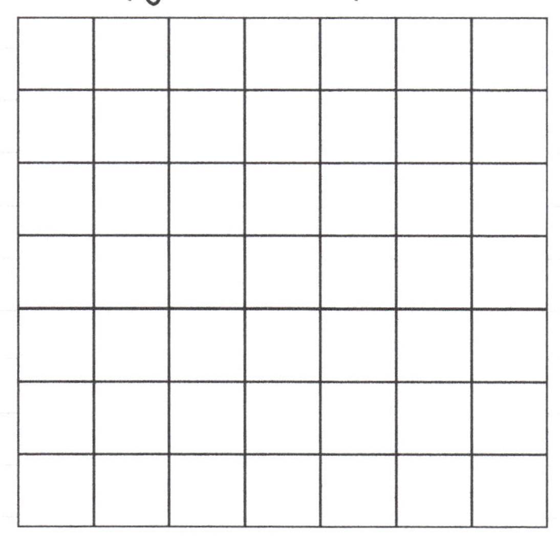

Sketch Code - 2

Bulls eye pattern code

Use the Blank Code blocks to copy the above pattern.

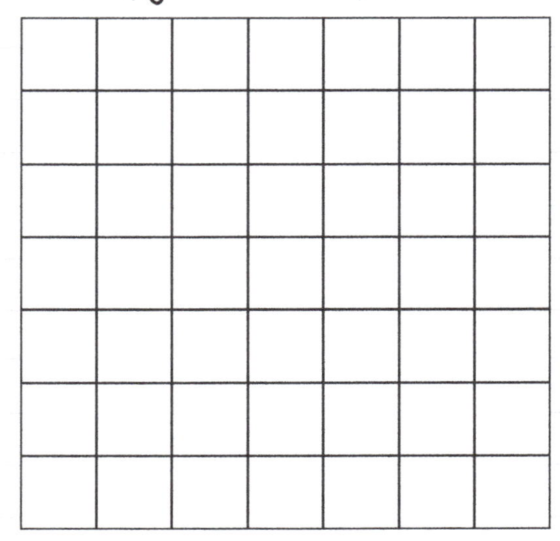

Sketch Code - 3

"Bad Detective Hat" pattern code

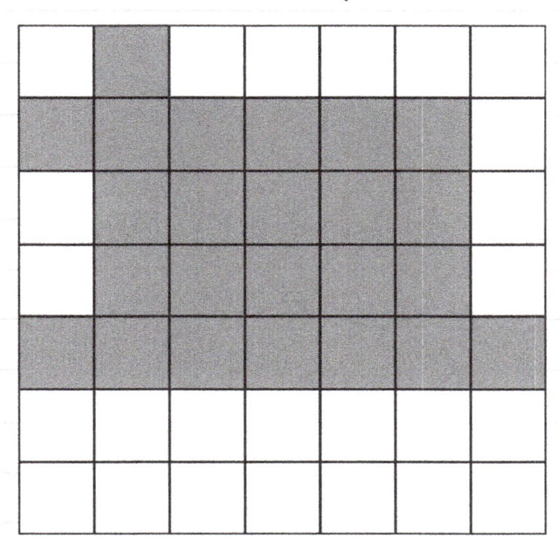

Use the Blank Code blocks to copy the above pattern.

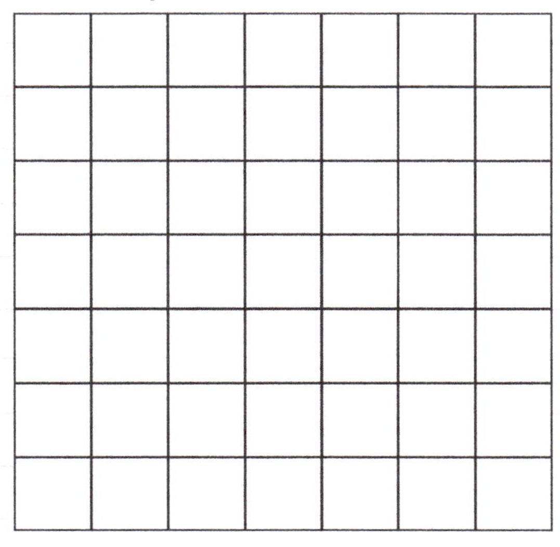

Those Sketch puzzles were a piece of [cake], right?

Now you can try your hand at these puzzles.

Word Puzzle 1

T R I I B O F N X L G A D Y P P A H L J
O I H X I Y U K M I Q H X I Q S O G R Y
W A J V X G N I R A D O D S M Y U E E P
Y K B F M G U W V S T S E N O H L N Q Z
L C V Y J D N I P I P J P G E D U U M G
I B V O Y O J L M G T K O O L Y F I F H
N D G O F J Q D C I T E G R E N E N A S
U Z K G R N B D K J G E I G R A P E B E
F V Y F I N V E L I R I Y E A M O V U B
C W I U E Y B T P Z A H N O E I H O L V
K E P N N M H E T R C Q F U X C M B O J
Y O N N D U R R R N I S A S C T G I U V
Z L J Y L A Z M K H O K U U I J V J S S
Q O G A Y U G I A Z U F N J T M Q S J A
K X K A L B O N E C S U O R E N E G R H
E V A R Q N Y E K G A E E W D E W P O N
P F O N U X X D K Q K G G R A T E F U L
F C A F C E X T R A O R D I N A R Y C X
C X H X A K O H Q N M U S W L L D T N J
N J Z A R C E F E A R L E S S C Y V J Q

DARING
DETERMINED
DYNAMIC
ENERGETIC
EXCITED
EXTRAORDINARY
FABULOUS
FEARLESS
FRIENDLY
FUN
FUNNY
GENEROUS
GENUINE
GORGEOUS
GRACIOUS
GRATEFUL
HAPPY
HONEST
HOPEFUL

Source: Teacherscorner.net

Answer on page: 204

Word Puzzle 2

R W J Y P T E U Q N V B R Y F G V W R N
O O H V R N V O J U E E A J N N W F V T
P R E X N U E C V L O Y A L Q O Y Y Z S
T R Z F C E L B A V O L D R B R Y H E G
I R L U F T H G I S N I P R D T N W P G
M V P H N X V Y I E T V A W R S R T Z P
I N T E L L I G E N T D S H H D D W K V
S U T D M U S I C A L A S C G K I V M Y
T H N S C C Y N X M T L I J U H I S A F
I C D M H V C D Z U V A O J W D P U E K
C B N U D V N E Q H Z T N B G I O O L R
S B I S T S E P A Q H S A X Q B F E B G
V B K P A T G E L I Y P T N F T Y N I S
L O I Y F Y A N F X U P E A O G H A D I
W I D B Q E Z D G C N U R R V B Y T E K
J A R E D E T E C T I V E D K R M N R R
L N P W B V F N K E A O Q J A L J O C E
R Y T N X B I T P F L O V I N G S P N K
K V A G V A G M U X D H N B A K L S I F
F O Z F C T T U J O Y F U L O V E D H P

AGENCY
DETECTIVE
INCREDIBLE
INDEPENDENT
INSIGHTFUL
INTELLIGENT
JOYFUL
KIND
LOVABLE
LOVED
LOVING
LOYAL
MUSICAL
OPTIMISTIC
PASSIONATE
SPONTANEOUS
SPY
STRONG

Source: Teacherscorner.net

Answer on page: 204

Word Puzzle 3

U A V I M O N J N Y T Y T Z S T N P N F
X L A V H G S U K O G N I R A C U W P V
P C I D S H E C O U R A G E O U S H G F
E Z Q X F T H Z G R J V X G B C O V Y H
Q D A D V E N T U R O U S E N R H M M D
I U A M A Z I N G I T B R D D E N C D K
W L K V W M M N Z K A D Q T G A I E R N
X W E T A R E D I S N O C M C T F O J C
T Q D P K H A M G W I M N S I I Q O Z J
P W P U J N X U T L T H T V G V F I R B
E Z G H M F C V D D H K P Z Z E P U P T
D E T A N O I S S A P M O C S P L D Z U
X P C Z O H N K V C G S B P U B Z H Q O
E V A R B X A J Q F K O Q D O Y E X X S
D I F V Z I S D M W F L H O I F R Q N R
I P O O B G L H M K R A Q H T Z U E Q W
X D F G X J Q S Q Y N M X R I G W E Q Y
V X J N W M W B W Z K I A U B L R U C R
N F Q N N Z A U V V T W A L M D K H Y B
Y U L A T G X P Q D I H T U A N L S L S

ADVENTUROUS	AMAZING	AMBITIOUS
BRAVE	CARING	COMPASSIONATE
CONSIDERATE	COURAGEOUS	CREATIVE

Source: Teacherscorner.net

Answer on page: 204

Word Puzzle 4

I O L O V E D X M B N J F K I G N U L A
N S C D U X L I O E Q Y P Q G Z Z T I O
D H N M Z J R I N C R E D I B L E M P C
E G T T X R G E F P J Q E N T T I A L L
P Z E J O G N I V O L P O S I T I V E E
E I Y R E U I S V M C N F I E F X R B F
N R R X U B R J M V I A H G E F Z S T T
D S U E Q A I O U U C Y C H W P D X F U
E N F A I W P I E G X V Y T O X P D I S
N L D R N Y S Z R F Z I Q F J M Z S Y K
T O G D U O N T J A W X W U G W Q Z P H
H P T N E G I L L E T N I L N H I G J G
Y T D N I K L O Y A L U L N O C O X H K
I I A O O R L L E N B E Y F N S M T A Y
J M I G A J T U Y P A S S I O N A T E V
B I Y N S R V F K U L A C I S U M C F Y
G S F O R M H Y D Z E E L B A V O L P N
O T W R R S P O N T A N E O U S S A O Q
F I X T G N N J L B S X J W O N A W C M
I C S S R K P W U W E O C P J H P L C Y

INCREDIBLE
INSPIRING
KIND
LOVING
OPTIMISTIC
SPONTANEOUS

INDEPENDENT
INTELLIGENT
LOVABLE
LOYAL
PASSIONATE
STRONG

INSIGHTFUL
JOYFUL
LOVED
MUSICAL
POSITIVE
UNIQUE

Source: Teacherscorner.net

Answer on page: 205

Word Puzzle 5

R C D D T L S W B Y M N O S T A W L M Q
O M J O D R N W R O Y N O Q E B V R W U
S A Y L L F Y B M N J C D K S A C W Y W
B K E K C O L R E H S I L C B M R I P H
D E T E C T G E G N Y Y M A W X W Q Z N
F R K F N S M P A U F J R V C O I Y C K
V M I Z X X J O D J I E B A C D Y J N G
A K F S T V H C V L N P Q W C S X R B C
G K D K M G U S W F G O F T C M J V P N
T P A M P L N E L J A C B Q I P K Q A U
N V L T S A K L W Z M S Y U X C Z U P H
E F G O A S Y E F N M O G C C F F F E R
G X O N L S V T M J R R H K A N E E R E
I Y R V J J O S R G E C U D E D U U N T
L Z I M S B D O N F J I P G R R K M D U
L A T Y K M T I H L E M T J A H E I N P
E O H B R A I N I A C M K L Z V S Q U M
T S M Q C K H H F I N G E R P R I N T O
N Q P E T C E F R E P C U I U I N D W C
I S N L D E D L N V E L D G P D K L V S

ALGORITHM
DEDUCE
GLASS
MAKER
PAPER
TELESCOPE
BRAINIAC
DETECT
INTELLIGENT
MAP
PERFECT
WATSON
COMPUTER
FINGERPRINT
MAGNIFY
MICROSCOPE
SHERLOCK

Source: Teacherscorner.net

Answer on page: 205

Word Puzzle 6

B	K	Z	X	H	X	W	G	B	Q	B	G	D	O	E	I	W	Y	U	C
U	H	D	M	E	G	A	R	U	O	C	N	E	X	N	V	N	W	X	T
D	D	Q	J	K	X	Q	O	N	P	J	R	H	V	O	S	L	F	C	W
M	M	L	G	T	G	M	R	F	I	R	I	I	F	N	E	Q	C	V	C
W	P	H	Y	N	I	E	Y	D	Z	L	G	Z	M	Q	I	H	M	V	C
D	W	S	M	T	T	J	F	T	A	O	U	H	N	X	Q	E	I	K	R
W	V	L	O	N	O	H	V	R	R	Q	L	W	O	F	P	N	N	D	P
L	Q	C	Z	L	L	O	A	A	V	Q	H	L	L	M	J	D	S	P	W
U	K	P	Y	C	R	T	T	E	N	I	M	A	X	E	I	U	W	B	G
V	T	J	P	B	E	E	M	U	B	D	K	Y	X	U	I	U	H	R	I
Y	D	B	A	E	Q	T	C	M	T	W	D	P	W	K	D	R	E	S	B
Q	D	Y	T	L	K	N	E	O	G	X	L	Y	W	O	B	V	P	W	D
X	Z	J	F	S	V	U	M	T	N	X	H	Z	E	F	O	S	F	X	S
P	W	S	S	J	V	A	E	N	O	N	O	K	M	C	L	P	S	T	S
I	I	W	F	E	G	V	T	E	Q	T	O	Y	S	K	U	D	J	M	D
S	J	G	Z	F	U	X	A	U	Y	C	M	I	Q	T	N	W	H	T	L
X	F	V	N	M	M	S	I	T	E	B	D	I	T	A	C	I	C	D	U
I	J	J	W	K	O	T	W	Q	G	H	Z	K	L	E	T	T	Z	N	R
S	L	D	A	V	P	G	U	G	U	O	C	R	D	M	R	T	E	X	T
D	Z	D	Q	O	V	E	J	V	W	Q	X	R	E	T	K	Y	D	N	F

ENCOURAGE
DISCOVER
RECONNOITER
EXHILARATE
EXAMINE
INVIGORATE
WITTY

Source: Teacherscorner.net

Answer on page: 205

Word Puzzle 7

```
E H W D J V M I K Y W F Z F S R Z I K D
E V W F A S U T C P W R M B X S I R D E
A Q C W G O F Z S C X W W E W X G C B L
A J H Y T L Y G H P E U V X L R O B F R
S X O T R G R B Q G D H E M U T L O C B
P P S T T P E L Z J S F I R N T N G R U
B M P K O Q A C H I E V E S V G R O H C
H Q O J X O A N L O K B C K X H U Z X T
R F E L A Y C P W A L H V H M I R N E S
O G X V B M M A N J Q B D I Z H F G X H
M Q X R S O E T B Y S C F Q C Q P C P S
S Y C I C U O T T M I K H Q D T I M E Y
D W J C D U K E G X N G I S E D C L Q H
D L A J B K I R G F E Y A E E R P B R W
U I O G D I E N Y C Q R R U E V T M Y H
O U Y F E P P F O A F I W B R V H Z H X
I I I R O T P E B L U E P R I N T Y K Z
P T Y Q P T Z Z N Q X O E Q T H R O L T
S O C D C D N A C Z X M G X G M N T K Q
O R H V M F B A P V P K Z L E W K H N E
```

PATTERN
DESIGN
ACCOMPLISH
ACHIEVE
BLUEPRINT
ACQUIRE
TIME

Source: Teacherscorner.net

Answer on page: 206

Word Puzzle 8

D R M B Q T W W I F Y D B Y G T H Z L U
B M Q A E I S C O K W L V M U B N F U D
D O B G S Z S Y X I W T Q W W Z O E F N
D T P Y I H W V E T D V K N D W J V R J
T E G A A U G G Z T U F C T N I S E E R
K C Y O R R A K I P A A H C M P Y V E G
V Z Y O S E U Y P K H V E R Q H O G H Q
T V W Y J D R N Y Y V D I J J R R W C P
C S C L B R U R J L N I Q T P O E I D R
F A S I H O E E K K V M F M L Q S T A X
W S F G R E S V U H G Q I W K U M L F Y
E W J H S U T O O A A G Y I P V C E E Z
B F Y N X J O C W G N M C S M Q D K T E
S S F A M M L W K A P Q E G B F P C A A
Y R X W Z V K Q T H W N M B Y Y K H E K
B N S I T C I V I I X Z R Z B T O W R R
K Z X C J M R N Q F F D C X T Y W I C E
S D N I B E Z C R K B F O N B Z V V G T
Z Q F T J Y R V O M G E A J H F Z P W P
P Q S L Z H M D Z O N A Y X K D E Z Q K

IMPROVE
COVER
OVERJOYED
CREATE
CULTIVATE
RAISE
CHEERFUL

Source: Teacherscorner.net

Answer on page: 206

Word Puzzle 9

U R R K Y B X M I I P Y G L U R M V S A
O X H V B H D Y H G E Y X E B X O S U M
N O H Q S K Z O J N J A H W H N F N O L
G G J Y K Q I M R I Y K P Z R S F X R G
Y N J C A P J V V M J M B M X Y N K O O
S N K X V R Z V D A X B K H M W V Q D G
K I S Q K M L A D E E M J W X U M L N S
M S S F Y J Z F Y L Z Z D G S A O I E A
W X J Q S Z Z X B G K R I M E V N T L I
T N Z A L H Q A Z J P M F A B N A O P I
C B F I K C R P L J W V W T I R S W S N
P R N S I O D R O D G G B H B A I U U D
R G B R M F D N L L Z V S E B H B G T O
O F I E F B V X W L U T L N H N G Z H G
H N M V E F A Z I V B E R C T V H T X T
L D T A U E J A T W C I S X L Z A P S R
S Y E X J R E W F C R P E P H A H U Y S
J E W C S N Z F M M M H A B I L Z T Y R
H J O V G K H V R A C K J V S B F M L A
F H B C Y B B B N Q M W L D J W A J C Z

BRIGHT
CELEBRATE
SHINNING
GLEAMING
DAZZLING
SPLENDOROUS
MEMORABLE

Source: Teacherscorner.net

Answer on page: 206

Word Puzzle 10

B C T L L H A F N J A W G T P A M K G Q
A B H Q Y Y D Y W H F L C K V L R Q T Q
Q A G L Q P G T Z L I E E M S U F U I T
K J I Q B F J G J T D R I Y J O Q B H I
L P R J F P B A T I O M R A D W L N V L
X Q B N C V D E H Y N T C C Z P L F I R
V V V K M O R W U I I X X P I M Z R V U
L Y V G P W N X F C E G C I P C P B I F
O J B L A Z E R H V S D H U E C K H D D
L B B N E P G P D X W Q N M W Q R K M X
S F V A T N E U Q O L E Z E R R U B F X
S Z C E P G Z E H S D A A Q A F A U X U
R U D M H C Q Q D L A P L S D T U A H J
X H P Q J P Q L O N S Y G Y I L L L X F
A W O C Q U V G C U B N L X E W J J K V
S M X T H Q C E V L S S J L N P D E A Q
E N T T G P O K F Z F B D G T D F R Y K
J P E I G P O D X T B Z I A H C X X B P
V B W C D J T I B L W K H A J F U G I Y
W Z U M J F A I R O T B J H G S E Z M M

BRIGHT
BLAZE
ELOQUENT
GLITTER
RADIENT
VIVID
GOLDEN

Source: Teacherscorner.net

Answer on page: 206

Now try sketching some pictures. The picture is incomplete, you will have to examine the picture to finish it.

SKETCH ART

Instructions

The right side of the picture is the exact same shape as the left side of the picture.

- Using color pencils or crayons, color in the right side of the picture.
- Color in the right side of the picture using the same colors that you see from the left side of the picture.
- **PRO TIP:** Don't color too hard or you may color over the puzzle on the next page.

STYLE

Sketch Art 1

Name: ______________________

Finish the puzzle

Color in the rest of the boxes uses the color that looks like the sun.

Sketch Art 2

Name: ____________________

Finish the puzzle

Fill in the **yellow** and **pink** squares on the right side of the picture to match the yellow and pink squares on the left side of the picture.

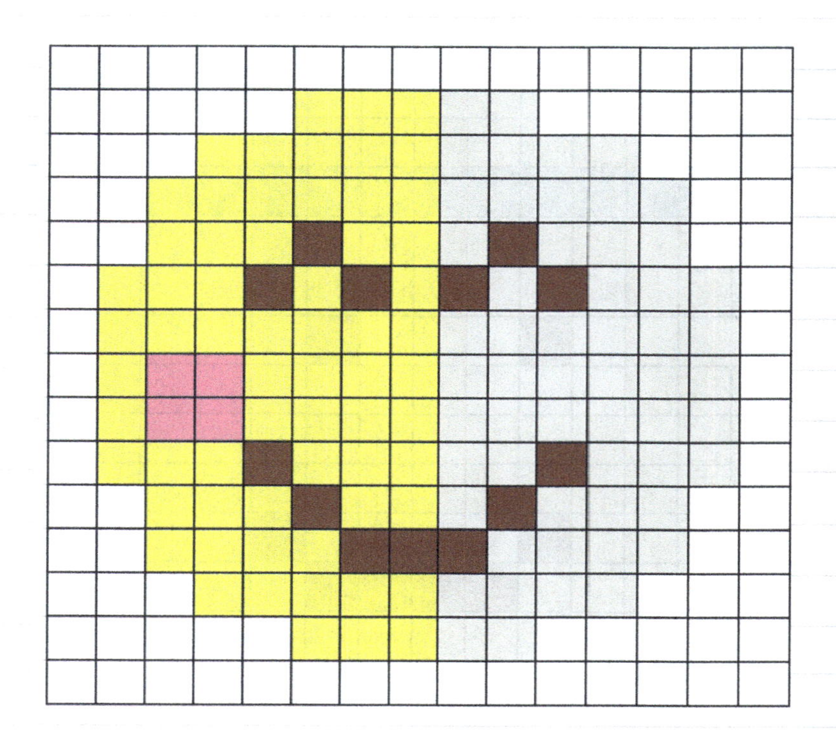

Sketch Art 3

Name: ____________________

Finish the puzzle

Fill in the yellow and blue squares on the right side of the picture to match the yellow and blue squares on the left side of the picture.

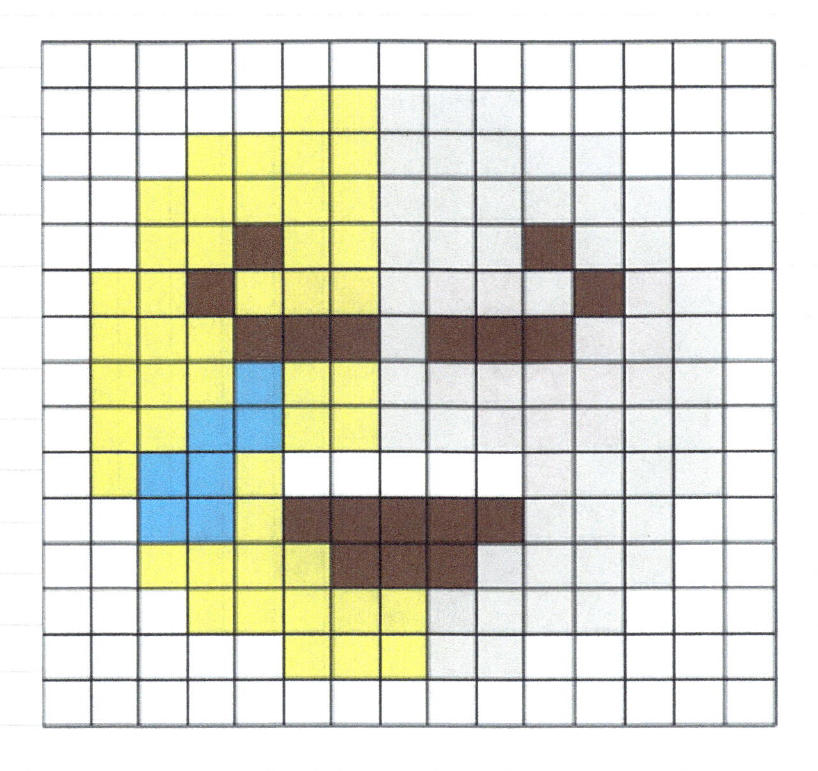

Sketch Art 4

Name: ____________________

Finish the puzzle

Fill in the **yellow** and **red** squares on the right side of the picture to match the **yellow** and **red** squares on the left side of the picture.

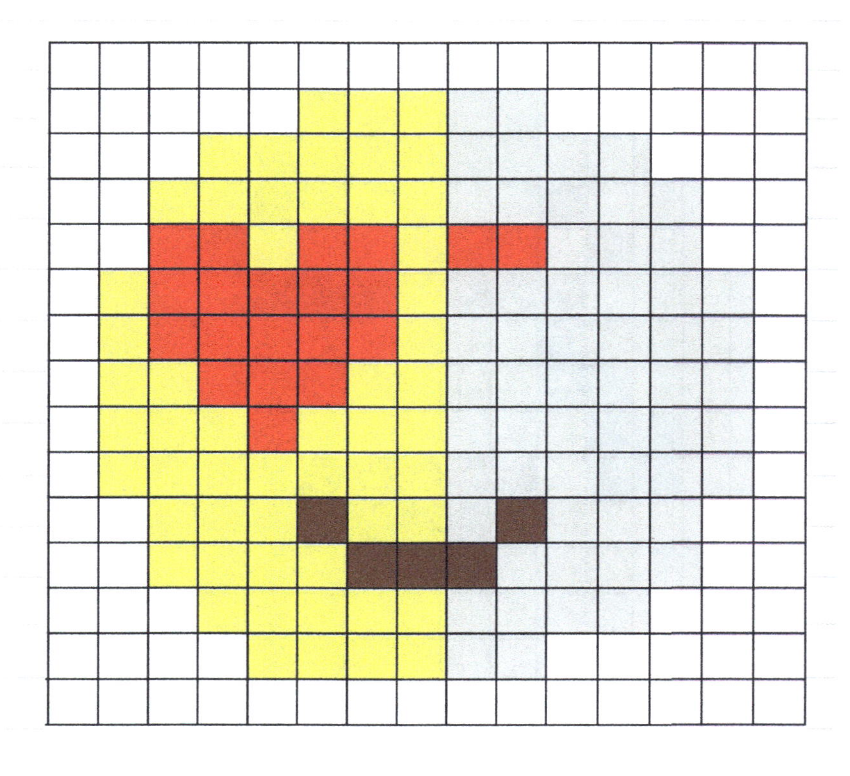

Sketch Art 5

Name: ______________________

Finish the puzzle

Fill in the yellow and black squares on the right side of the picture to match the yellow and black squares on the left side of the picture.

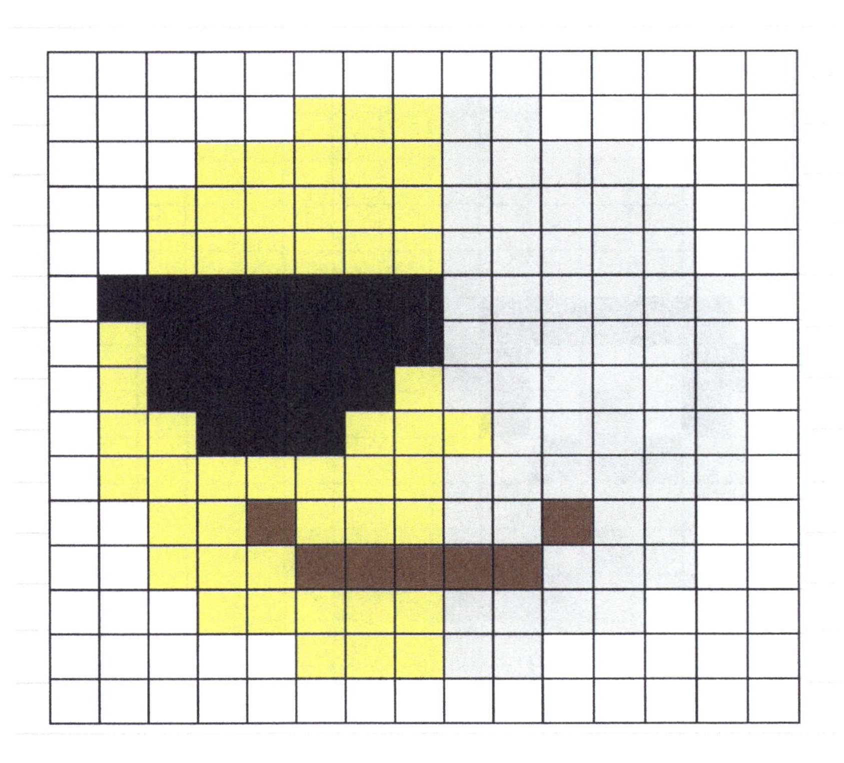

Sketch Art 6

Name: ______________________

Finish the puzzle

Fill in the **yellow** and **purple** squares on the right side of the picture to match the **yellow** and **purple** squares on the left side of the picture.

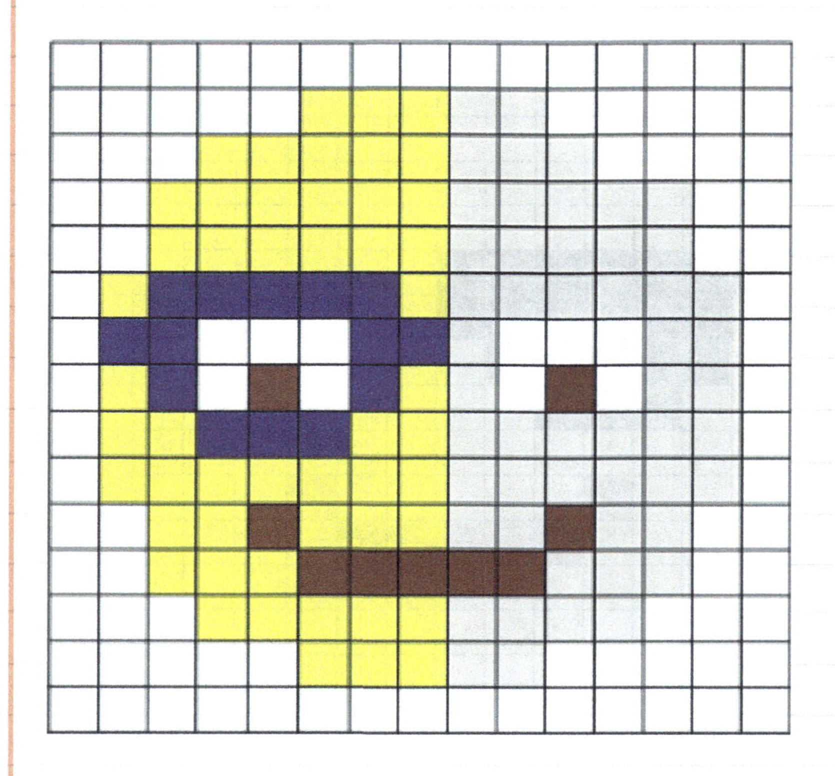

Sketch Art 7

Name: ______________________

Finish the puzzle

Fill in the yellow and brown squares on the right side of the picture to match the yellow and brown squares on the left side of the picture.

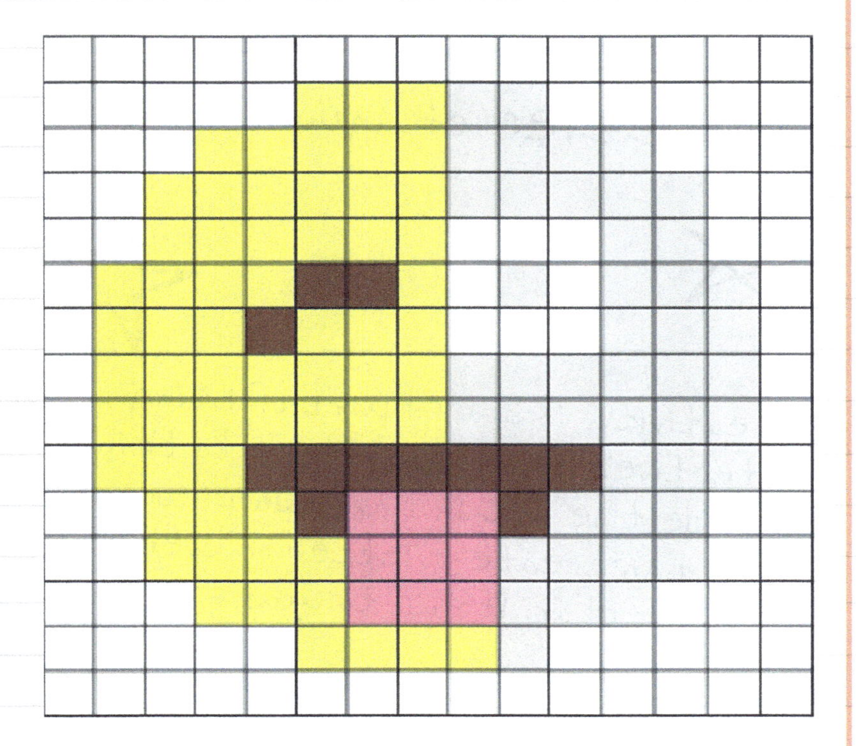

BE CREATIVE

Create some sketch puzzles of your own.

Creativity is a BIG part of being a detective. We always have to think outside the box. In your own pictures you can create a letter or even a star. It's up to you!

Design Art 1

Name: ____________________

Create your own Picture

Use the below boxes to color in your own picture design.

Design Art 2

Name: ____________________

Create your own Picture

Use the below boxes to color in your own picture design.

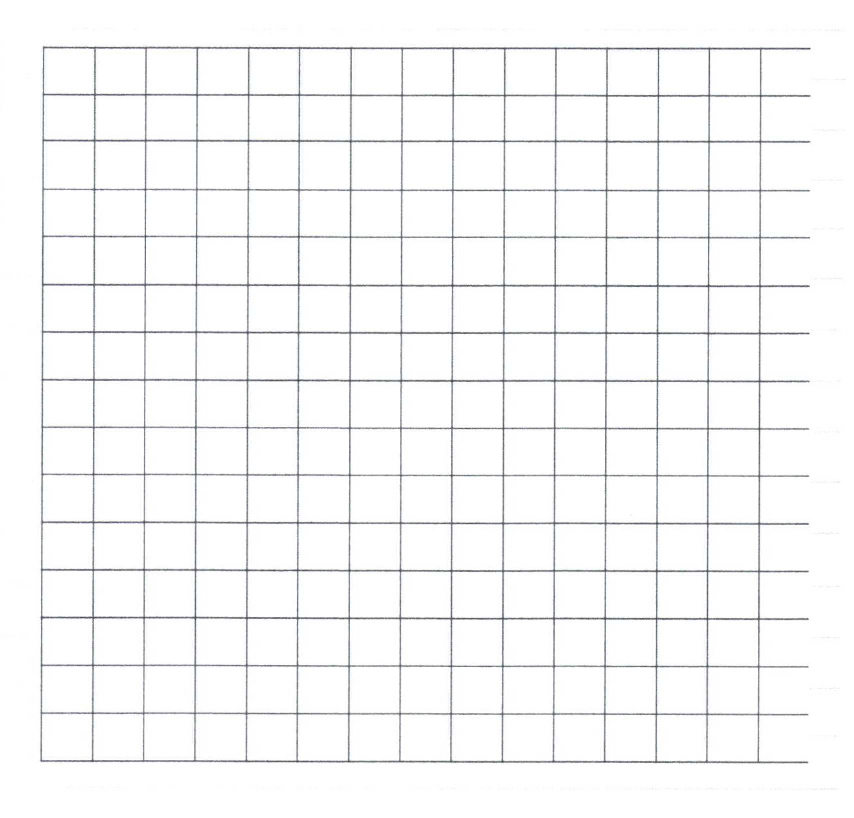

Design Art 3

Name: ____________________

Create your own Picture

Use the below boxes to color in your own picture design.

Design Art 4

Name: ______________________

Create your own Picture

Use the below boxes to color in your own picture design.

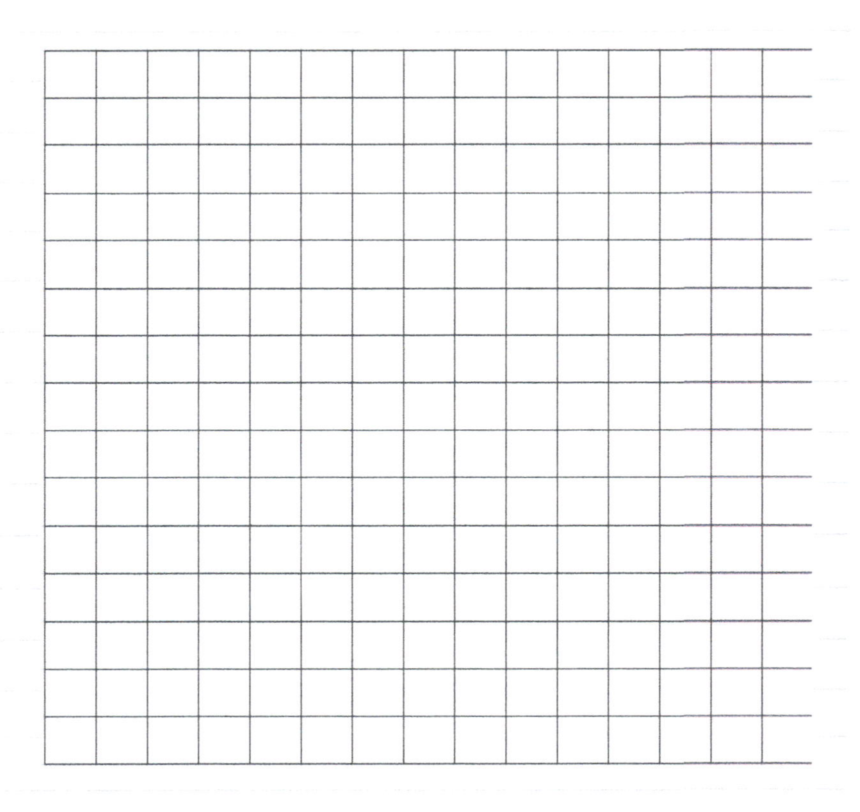

Design Art 5

Name: ______________________

Create your own Picture

Use the below boxes to color in your own picture design.

ABSTRACTION FUN

Fun Fact!

Did you know? Pablo Picasso used abstraction in his paintings. He painted abstract portraits of faces that did not look like a face, but you could recognize the face because it had the parts that complete a face (eyes, mouth, ears) so anyone could recognize it was a face. (1)

Abstraction puzzles!

The Abstraction puzzles will allow you to focus on what's important in the puzzle in order to complete it.

On the next few pages you must find what is important in the puzzle to complete the riddle.

Pssst.... Here's the answer to one riddle. The puzzle has BIRD in capital letters so it means "BIG BIRD".

Have fun! I know you'll solve them all without looking at the answers... you can always ask a friend or parent if you need help.

2+2=4

Rebus - 1

BIRD

What's your answer?

Source: Teacherscorner.net

Answer on page: 207

Rebus - 2

CUT

CUT CUT CUT

What's your answer?

Answer on page: 207

Rebus - 3

_ _ _ _ _ _ _ _ 

What's your answer?

Source:Teacherscorner.net

Answer on page: 207

Rebus - 4

B
BOW
W

What's your answer?

Answer on page: 207

Rebus - 5

GET

IT

What's your answer?

Source: Teacherscorner.net

Answer on page: 207

Rebus - 6

GO IT IT IT IT

What's your answer?

Answer on page: 207

Rebus - 7

ICE 3

What's your answer?

Source: Teacherscorner.net

Answer on page: 213

Rebus - 8

M1LLION

What's your answer?

Answer on page: 213

Rebus - 9

SITTING
THE WORLD

What's your answer?

Source: Teacherscorner.net

Answer on page: 213

Rebus - 10

TIME TIME

What's your answer?

Answer on page: 213

Rebus - 11

222 Day

What's your answer?

Source: Teacherscorner.net

Answer on page: 213

Rebus - 12

CHA WHO WHO RGE

What's your answer?

Answer on page: 213

Here are a few art puzzles for you to solve...

Using the color code below each picture, color in the number.

* For example in the puzzle on the next page
    * 1 = Teal or light green.
    * Everywhere you see a 1, color in the box with teal or light green.

Pixel Art 1

Name: ______________________

Color in the boxes below using the color code:

- ~ 1 = Teal or Green
- ~ 2 = Yellow
- ~ 3 = Brown

		1	1	1	2	2	2	2	2	2	1	1	1	
	1		2	2	2	2	2	2	2	2	2	2		1
		1	1	1	1	1	1	1	1	1	1	1	1	
		2	2	2	2	2	2	2	2	2	2	2		
	2	2	2				2				2	2	2	
	2	2	2		3		2		3		2	2	2	
	2	2	2				2				2	2	2	
	2	2	2	2	2	2	2	2	2	2	2	2	2	
	2	2	2	2	2	2	2	2	2	2	2	2	2	
		2	2	2	3					3	2	2		
		2	2	2	2	3	3	3	3	2	2	2		
			2	2	2	2	2	2	2	2	2			
					2	2	2	2	2					

1   2   3

Pixel Art 2

Name: ____________________

Color in the boxes below using the color code:

- 1 = Pink
- 2 = Yellow
- 3 = Brown

					2	2	2	2	2					
			2	2	2	2	2	2	2	2	2			
		2	2	2	2	2	2	2	2	2	2	2		
		2	2	2	2	2	2				2	2		
	2	2	2	2	3	3	2		3		2	2	2	
	2	2	2	3	2	2	2				2	2	2	
	2	2	2	2	2	2	2	2	2	2	2	2	2	
	2	2	2	2	2	2	2	2	2	2	2	2	2	
	2	2	2	3	3	3	3	3	3	3	2	2	2	
		2	2	2	3	1	1	1	3	2	2	2		
		2	2	2	2	1	1	1	2	2	2	2		
			2	2	2	1	1	1	2	2	2			
					2	2	2	2	2					

1 2 3

Pixel Art 3

Name: ____________________

Color in the boxes below using the color code:

~ 1 = Pink
~ 2 = Yellow
~ 3 = Brown

					2	2	2	2	2					
			2	2	2	2	2	2	2	2	2			
		2	2	2	2	2	2	2	2	2	2	2		
		2	2	2	3	2	2	2	3	2	2	2		
	2	2	2	3	2	3	2	3	2	3	2	2	2	
	2	2	2	2	2	2	2	2	2	2	2	2	2	
	2	1	1	2	2	2	2	2	2	2	1	1	2	
	2	1	1	2	2	2	2	2	2	2	1	1	2	
	2	2	2	3	2	2	2	2	2	3	2	2	2	
		2	2	2	3	2	2	2	3	2	2	2		
		2	2	2	2	3	3	3	2	2	2	2		
			2	2	2	2	2	2	2	2	2			
					2	2	2	2	2					

1 2 3

Pixel Art 4

Name: ______________________

Color in the boxes below using the color code:

~ 1 = Blue
~ 2 = Yellow
~ 3 = Brown

					2	2	2	2	2					
			2	2	2	2	2	2	2	2	2			
		2	2	2	2	2	2	2	2	2	2	2		
		2	2	3	2	2	2	2	2	3	2	2		
	2	2	3	2	2	2	2	2	2	2	3	2	2	
	2	2	2	3	3	3	2	3	3	3	2	2	2	
	2	2	2	1	2	2	2	2	2	1	2	2	2	
	2	2	1	1	2	2	2	2	2	1	1	2	2	
	2	1	1	2						2	1	1	2	
		1	1	2	3	3	3	3	3	2	1	1		
		2	2	2	2	3	3	3	2	2	2	2		
			2	2	2	2	2	2	2	2	2			
					2	2	2	2	2					

1 2 3

Pixel Art 5

Name: ______________________

Color in the boxes below using the color code:

- 1 = Red
- 2 = Yellow
- 3 = Brown

					2	2	2	2	2					
			2	2	2	2	2	2	2	2	2			
		2	2	2	2	2	2	2	2	2	2	2		
		1	1	2	1	1	2	1	1	2	1	1		
	2	1	1	1	1	1	2	1	1	1	1	1		
	2	1	1	1	1	1	2	1	1	1	1	1	2	
	2	2	1	1	1	2	2	2	1	1	1	2	2	
	2	2	2	1	2	2	2	2	2	1	2	2	2	
	2	2	2	2	2	2	2	2	2	2	2	2	2	
		2	2	2	3	2	2	2	3	2	2	2		
		2	2	2	2	3	3	3	2	2	2	2		
			2	2	2	2	2	2	2	2	2			
				2	2	2	2	2	2					

1 2 3

Pixel Art 6

Name: ______________________

Color in the boxes below using the color code:

- 1 = Black
- 2 = Yellow
- 3 = Brown

					2	2	2	2	2					
			2	2	2	2	2	2	2	2	2			
		2	2	2	2	2	2	2	2	2	2	2		
		2	2	2	2	2	2	2	2	2	2	2		
	1	1	1	1	1	1	1	1	1	1	1	1	1	
	2	1	1	1	1	1	1	1	1	1	1	1	2	
	2	1	1	1	1	1	2	1	1	1	1	1	2	
	2	2	1	1	1	2	2	2	1	1	1	2	2	
	2	2	2	2	2	2	2	2	2	2	2	2	2	
		2	2	3	2	2	2	2	2	3	2	2		
		2	2	2	3	3	3	3	3	2	2	2		
			2	2	2	2	2	2	2	2	2			
					2	2	2	2	2					

1 2 3

Pixel Art 7

Name: ____________________

Color in the boxes below using the color code:

- ~ 1 = Yellow
- ~ 2 = Orange
- ~ 3 = Brown

					1	1	1	1	1					
			1	1	1	1	1	1	1	1	1			
		1	1	1	1	1	1	1	1	1	1	1		
		1	1	3	1	1	1	1	1	3	1	1		
	1	1	1	1	3	1	1	1	3	1	1	1	1	
	1	1	1	3	1	1	1	1	1	3	1	1	1	
	1	1	1	1	1	1	1	1	1	1	1	1	1	
	1	1	1	1	1	1	1	1	1	1	1	1	1	
	1	1	1	3	3	3	3	3	3	3	1	1	1	
		1	1	1	3	2	2	2	3	1	1	1		
		1	1	1	1	2	2	2	1	1	1	1		
			1	1	1	2	2	2	1	1	1			
					1	1	1	1	1					

1   2   3

Pixel Art 8

Name: ____________________

Color in the boxes below using the color code:

- ~ 1 = Blue
- ~ 2 = Yellow
- ~ 3 = Brown

					2	2	2	2	2					
			2	2	2	2	2	2	2	2	2			
		2	2	2	2	2	2	2	2	2	2	2		
		2	2	3	2	2	2	2	2	3	2	2		
	2	2	3	2	2	2	2	2	2	2	3	2	2	
	2	2	2	3	3	2	2	2	3	3	2	2	2	
	2	2	2	1	1	2	2	2	1	1	2	2	2	
	2	2	2	1	1	2	2	2	1	1	2	2	2	
	2	2	2	1	1	2	2	2	1	1	2	2	2	
		2	2	1	1	2	3	2	1	1	2	2		
		2	2	1	1	2	2	2	1	1	2	2		
			2	2	2	2	2	2	2	2	2			
					2	2	2	2	2					

1 2 3

Pixel Art 9

Name: ____________________

Color in the boxes below using the color code:

- 1 = Yellow
- 2 = Brown

					1	1	1	1	1					
			1	1	1	1	1	1	1	1	1			
		1	1	1	1	1	1	1	1	1	1	1		
		1	1	2	2	1	1	1	2	2	1	1		
	1	1	2	1	1	2	1	2	1	1	2	1	1	
	1	1	1	1	1	1	1	1	1	1	1	1	1	
	1	2	2	2	2	2	2	2	2	2	2	2	1	
	1	2										2	1	
	1	2										2	1	
		1	2									1		
		1	1	2							1	1		
			1	1	2	2	2	2	2	1	1			
					1	1	1	1	1					

1 (yellow) 2 (brown)

Pixel Art 10

Name: ____________________

Color in the boxes below using the color code:

- ~ 1 = Blue or Green
- ~ 2 = Yellow
- ~ 3 = Brown

					2	2	1	1	1					
			2	2	2	2	2	2	1	2	2			
		2	2	2	2	2	2	1	2	2	1	1	1	
		1	1	1	1	1	2	2	2	2	2	2	1	
	1	1	1	1	1	1	2	2	2	1	1	2	1	
	1	1	1	1	1	1	1	1	1	1	2	1	1	
	1	1	1	3	3	1	1	1	3	3	2	2	2	
	1	1	1	1	1	1	1	1	1	1	1	1	1	
	1	1	1	1	1	1	1	1	1	1	1	1	1	
		1	1	1	1	1	1	1	1	1	2	2	2	
		1	1	1	1	1	3	1	1	1	1	1	2	
			1	1	1	1	1	1	1	1	1	2		
					1	1	1	1	1		2			
											2	2	2	

1 2  3

Pixel Art 11

Name: ____________________

Color in the boxes below using the color code:

- 1 = Black
- 2 = Yellow
- 3 = Red

							1	1	1	1	1	1								
					1	1	2	2	2	2	2	2	1	1						
				1	2	2	2	2	2	2	2	2	2	2	1					
			1	2	2	2	2	1	1	2	2	1	2	2	2	1				
		1	2	2	1	2	1	2	2	2	2	2	1	2	2	2	1			
		1	2	2	1	1	1	1	1	2	2	2	1	2	2	2	1			
	1	2	2	1	1	2	1	1	2	2	2	2	1	1	2	2	2	1		
	1	2	1	2	2	2	2	2	1	2	2	2	1	1	1	2	2	1		
		2	2	2	2	2	2	2	2	2	2	2	1	1	1	2	2	1		
	1	2	2	2	2	2	2	2	2	2	2	1	1	1	1	2	2	1		
	1	1	2	2	2	2	2	2	2	2	2	1	1	1	2	2	2	1		
	1	2	1	1	1	1	1	1	1	1	3	3	1	1	2	2	2	1		
		1	2	1	1	1	1	1	3	3	3	1	1	2	2	2	1			
		1	2	2	1	1	1	3	3	3	3	1	2	2	2	2	1			
			1	2	2	1	1	1	1	1	2	2	2	2	2	1				
				1	2	2	2	2	2	2	2	2	2	2	1					
					1	1	2	2	2	2	2	2	1	1						
							2	2	2	2	2	2								

1 ■ 2 ■ 3 ■

PATTERN FUN

Fun Fact!

Did you know? Even animals have patterns. The veiled chameleon is a species of chameleon native to the Arabian Peninsula in Yemen and Saudi Arabia. The Chameleon has a pattern on their bodies that allows them to change colors to match their background - They can become invisible! They can change color when they need to. (2)

Pattern Puzzles!

In the next few puzzles you'll have to figure out the pattern in order to solve the puzzle.

You're moving fast! we knew you were a GENIUS! You're sooo close to the end.

Now you can take on the pattern puzzles. Get through these mazes as fast as you can.

Maze - 1

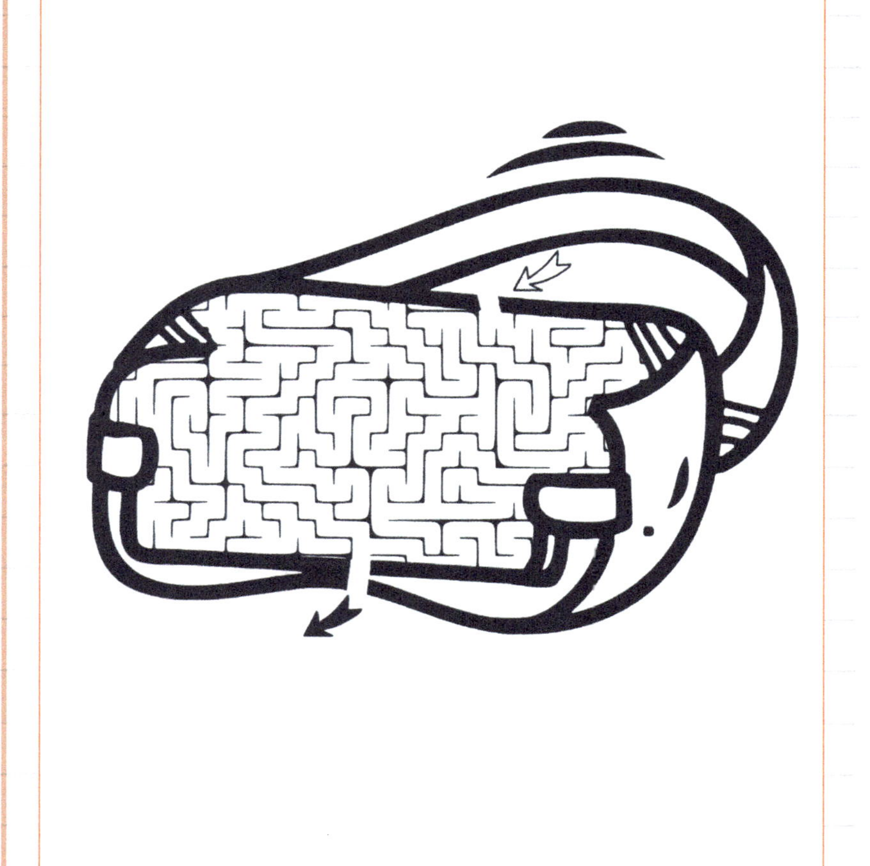

Answer on page: 210

Maze - 2

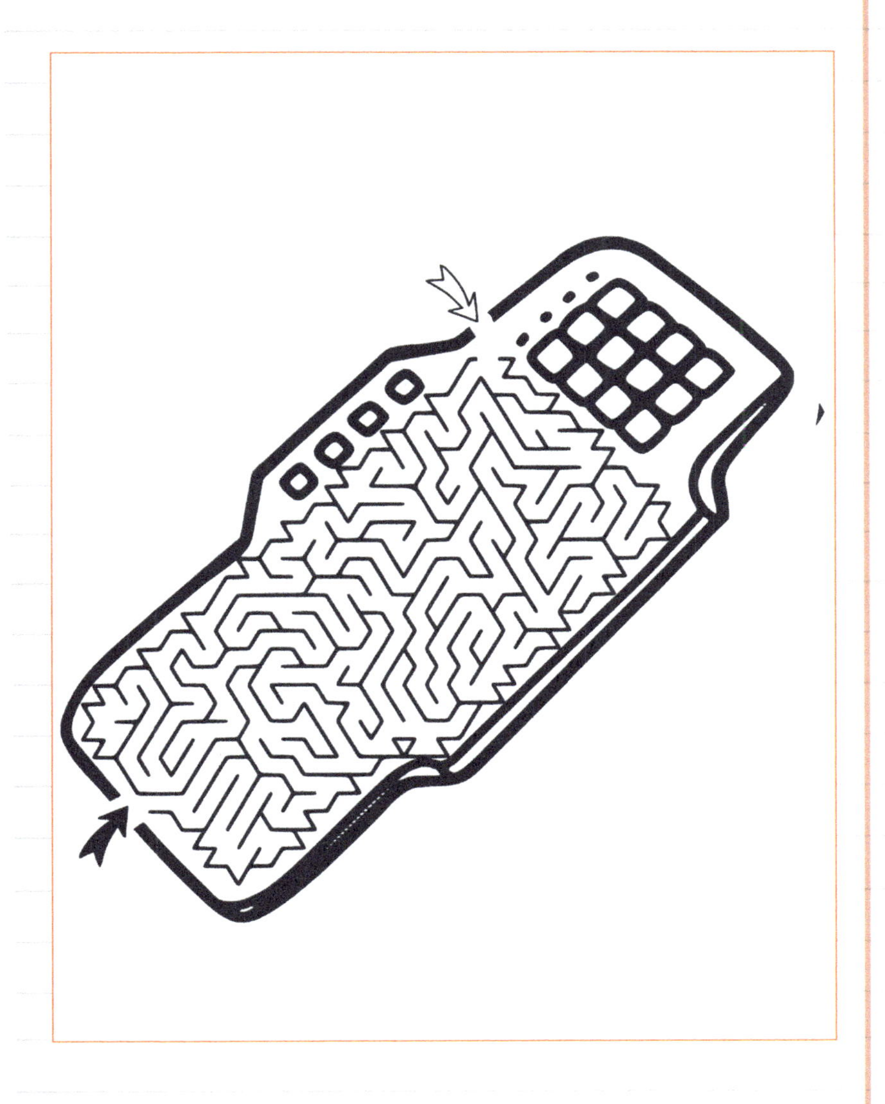

Answer on page: 210

Maze - 3

Answer on page: 210

Maze - 4

Answer on page: 210

Maze - 5

Answer on page: 210

Maze - 6

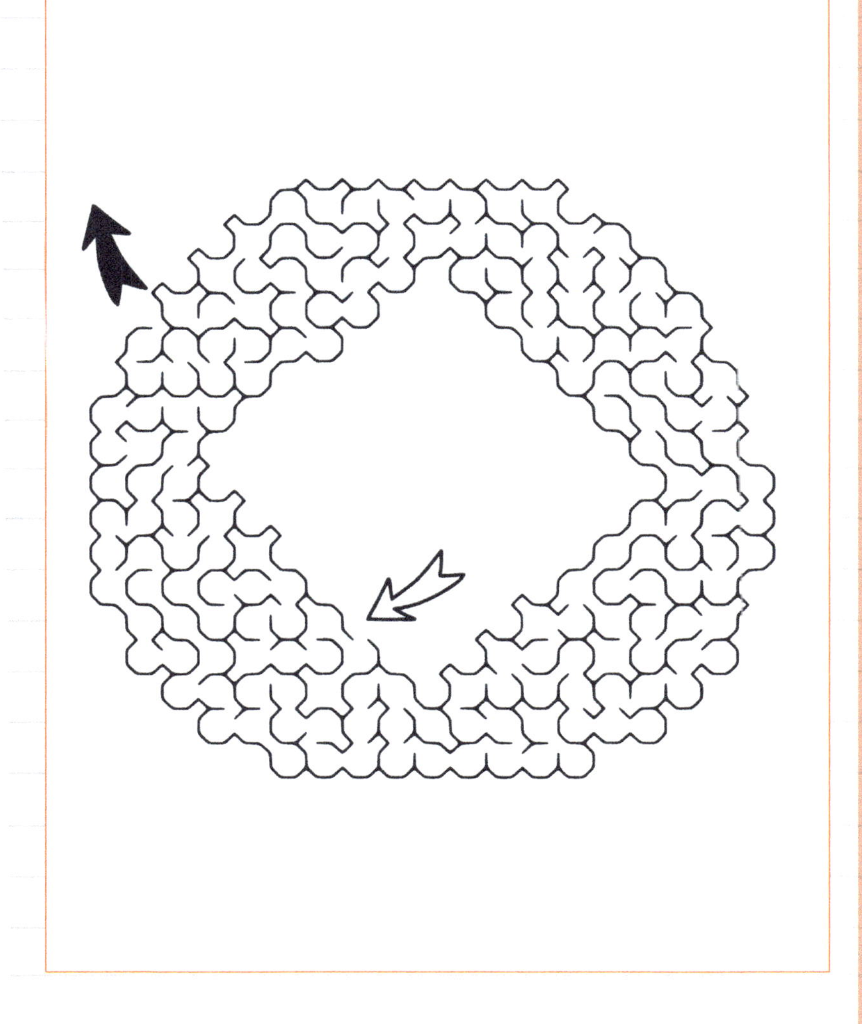

Answer on page: 210

Maze - 7

Answer on page: 210

Maze - 8

Answer on page: 211

Maze - 9

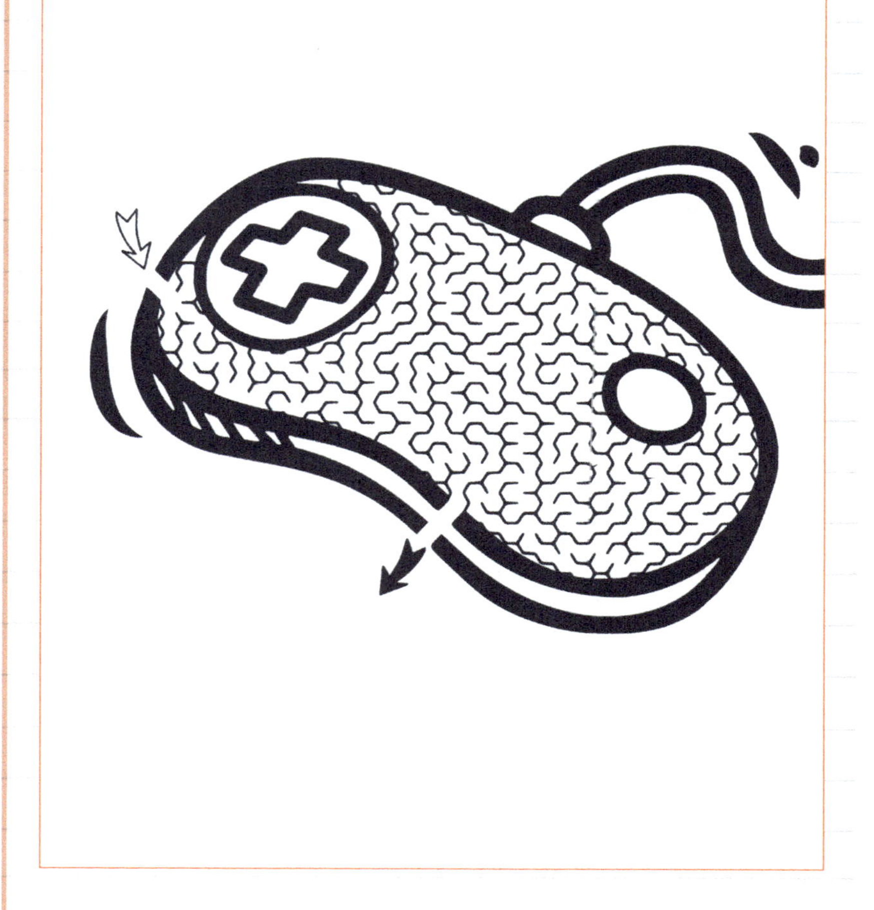

Answer on page: 211

Maze - 10

Answer on page: 211

Maze - 11

Answer on page: 211

Maze - 12

Answer on page: 211

Maze - 13

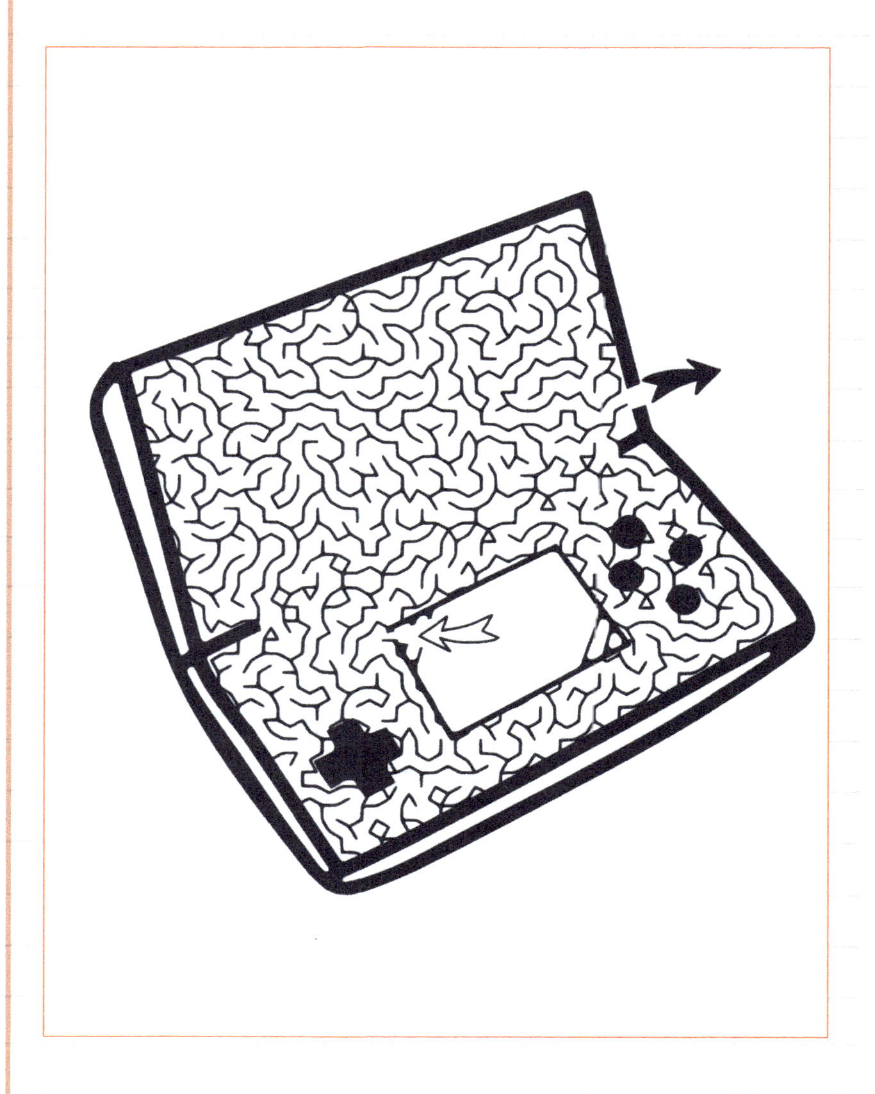

Answer on page: 211

Maze - 14

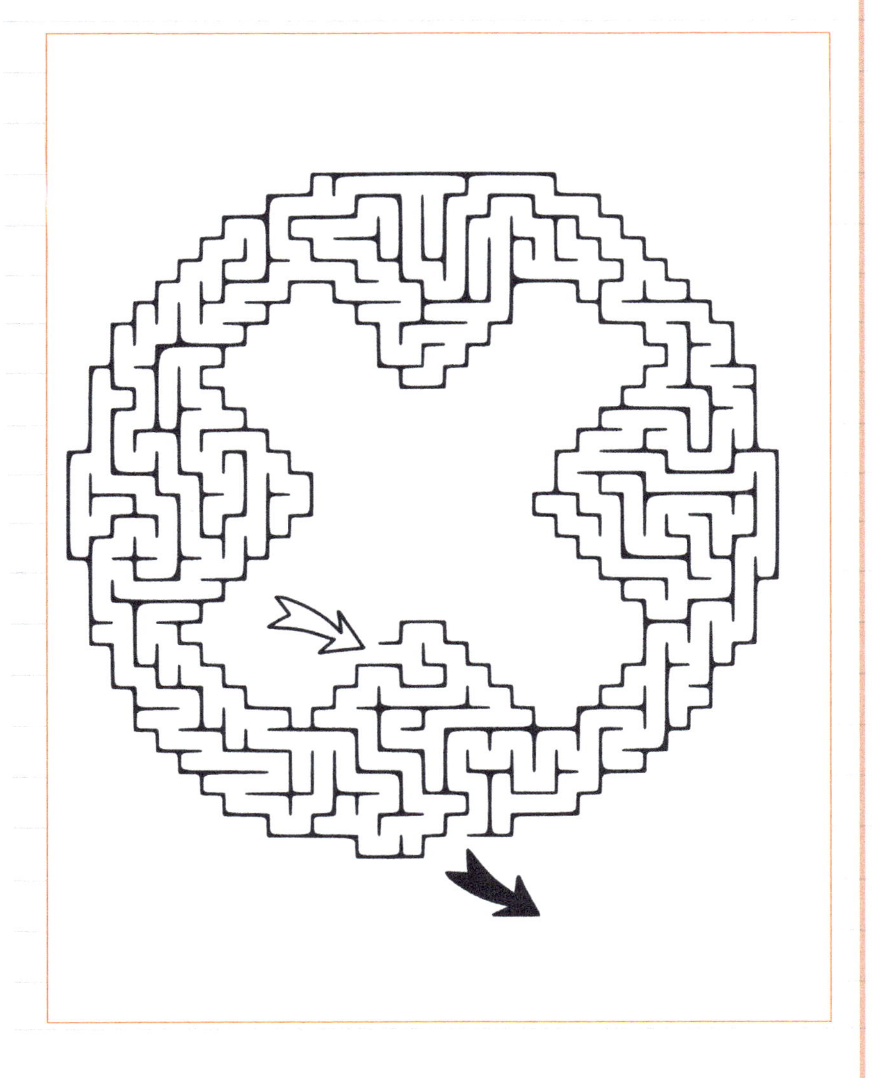

Answer on page: 212

Maze - 15

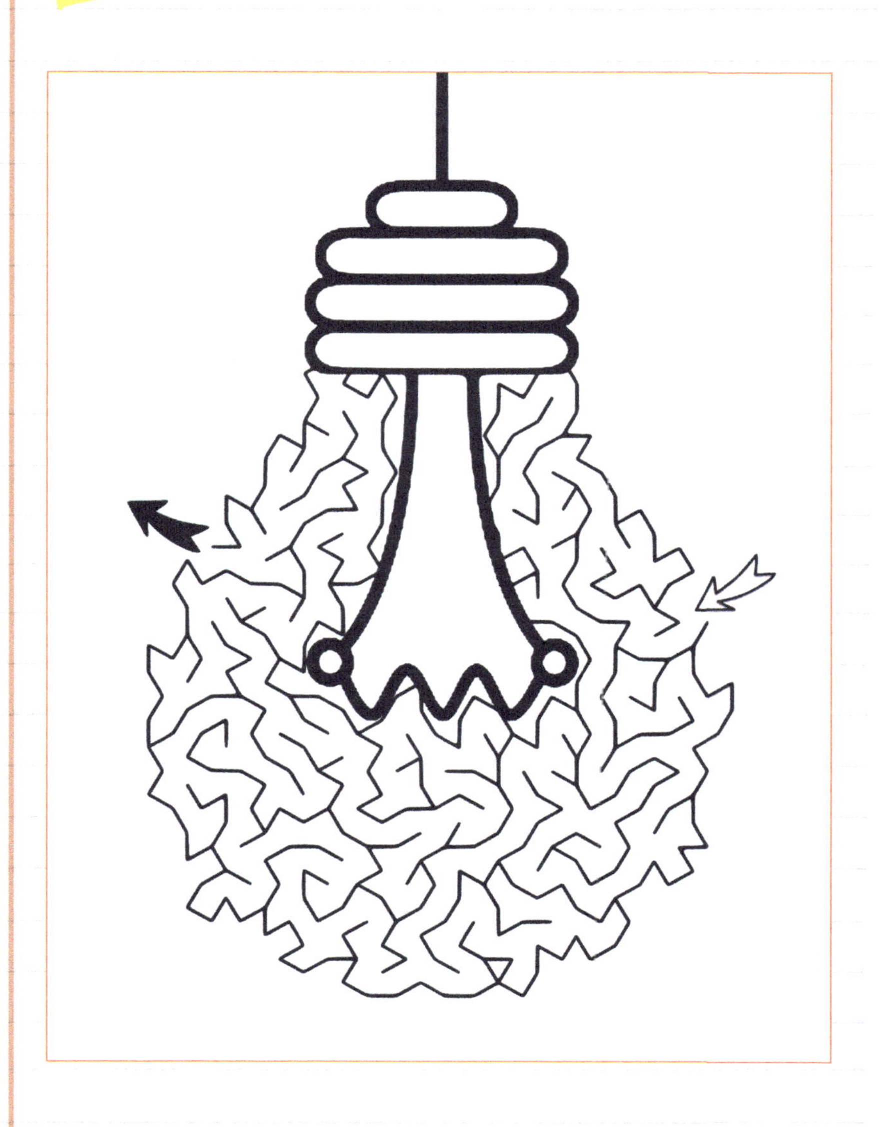

Answer on page: 212

Maze - 16

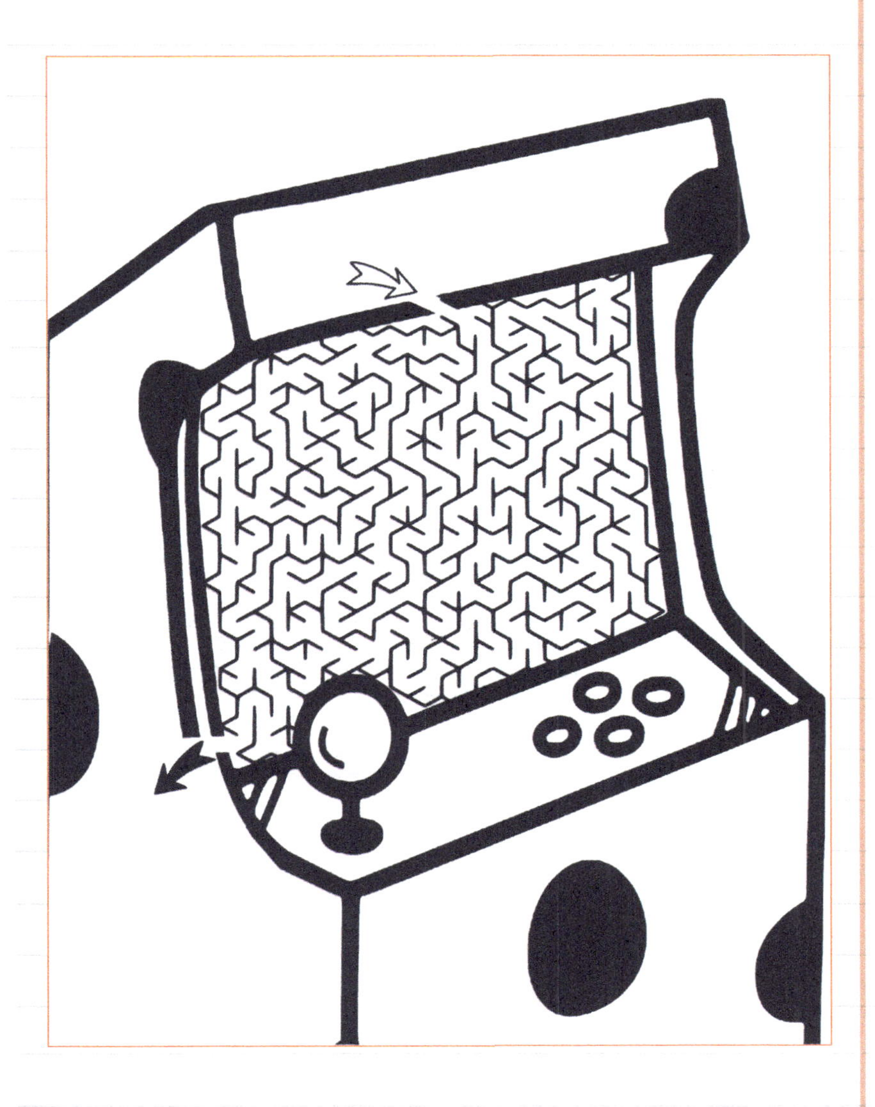

Answer on page: 212

Maze - 17

Answer on page: 212

Maze - 18

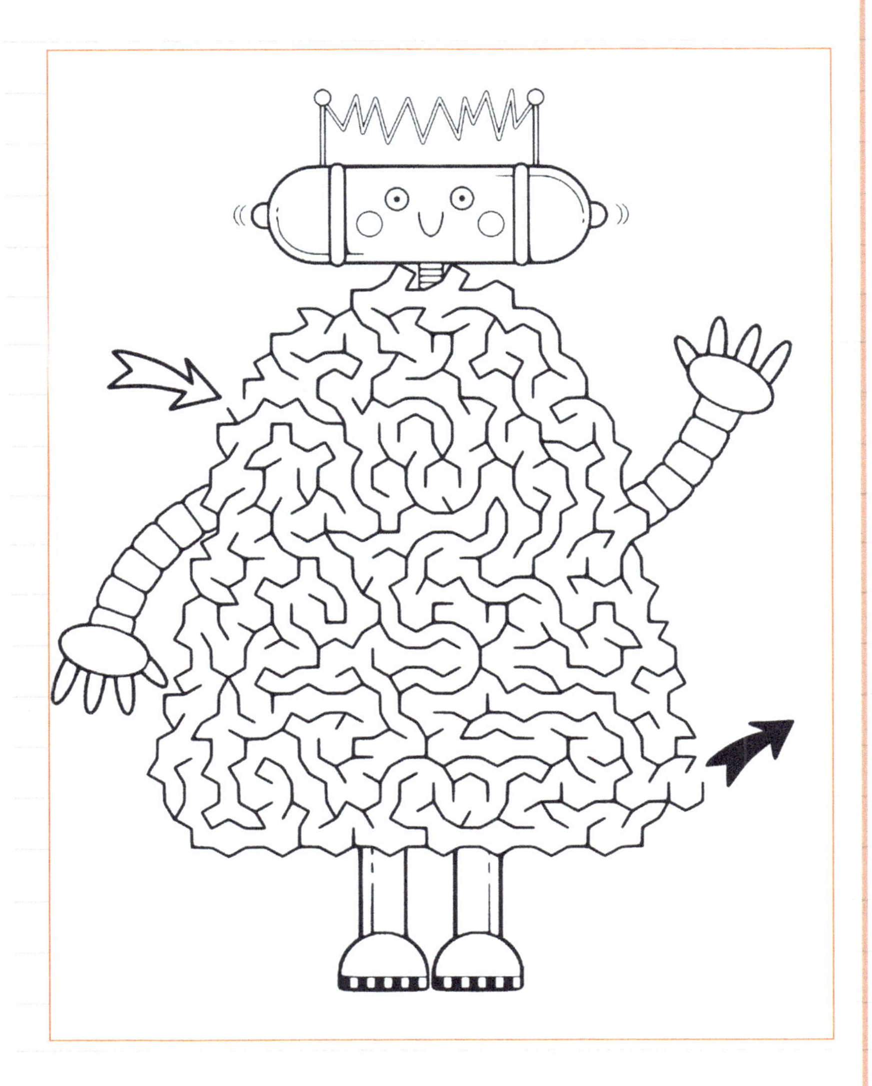

Answer on page: 212

Maze - 19

Answer on page: 212

Maze - 20

Answer on page: 212

Riddle

The tomato woke up from his nap simmering because a big hairy hand almost squeezed the juice out of him. "Owwww" protested the tomato. The person the hand belonged to paid him no attention and tossed him back into the pile. This was simply getting out of hand.

"We have to do something; we have to fight back." Thomas the tomato called to his friend across the aisle. Kyle the cucumber rolled over "well we've been talking about a fruits and vegetable strike".

Later that day Thomas the tomato was stewing. There were 3 tomatoes that were squeezed to the point of no return and the poor celery had been stripped bare to the bone.

"Aren't we tired of being treated with no respect!" Yelled Thomas.... all the other fruits and vegetables yelled "Yeah"

"We have something to say to these humans. Carrots, apples, celery, squash, lettuce, and bananas gather up. We're going to send a message to the humans."

They gathered together and formed a message.

What do you think they said?

SOLVING THE RIDDLE:

In the "Answer" section below:

* Unscrable the words in pink.
* Finish the words in black.

Answer?

llet uyo

Lettuce _ _ _ _ _ _ _
some_ _ _ _ ....
Treat us bet_ _ _ or we'll make
like a ba_ _ _ _ and spl_ t.

Answer on page: 208

And... here are some fart jokes... Solve the cryptograms to finish the joke.

Each number in a cryptogram puzzle represents a letter.

For example, on the next page :

- *A = 23, C = 3*

In the "Crytogram Key" section you will find the letter that corresponds to a number.

In the "Answer" section for each blank box write the letter that corresponds to the number.

Joke - 1

Wow, did you just fart?

* Solve the Crytogram puzzle to finish the joke.

CRYPTOGRAM KEY:

A	B	C	D	E	F	G	H	I	J	K	L	M
23	7	3		20				10			24	

N	O	P	Q	R	S	T	U	V	W	X	Y	Z
22	17				6	18	1		4		25	

ANSWER:

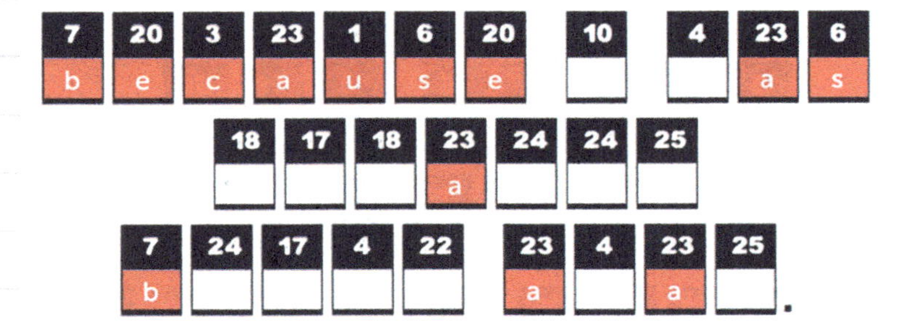

7	20	3	23	1	6	20		10		4	23	6
b	e	c	a	u	s	e					a	s

18	17	18	23	24	24	25
			a			

7	24	17	4	22		23	4	23	25
b						a		a	.

Answer on page: 213

Joke - 2

You think you have it rough!

* Solve the Crytogram puzzle to finish the joke

CRYPTOGRAM KEY

A	B	C	D	E	F	G	H	I	J	K	L	M
19		14	24	7	6		4	12		16	22	1

N	O	P	Q	R	S	T	U	V	W	X	Y	Z
5	11			21	10	3	25		20		23	

ANSWER:

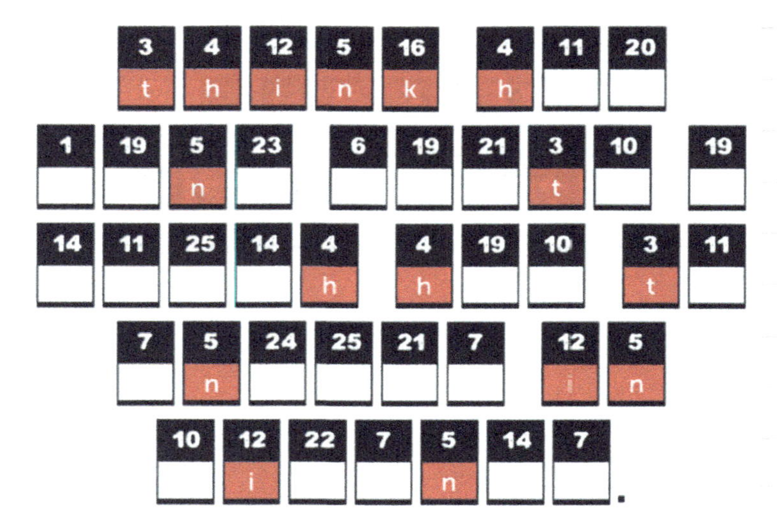

Answer on page: 213

Joke - 3

And.... the ideal weight of a fart is?

* Solve the Crytogram puzzle to finish the joke

CRYPTOGRAM KEY

A	B	C	D	E	F	G	H	I	J	K	L	M
	17	24	22		11	4	12		8	23	14	18

N	O	P	Q	R	S	T	U	V	W	X	Y	Z
25		2	5	16	6	26		7	20	1	3	10

ANSWER:

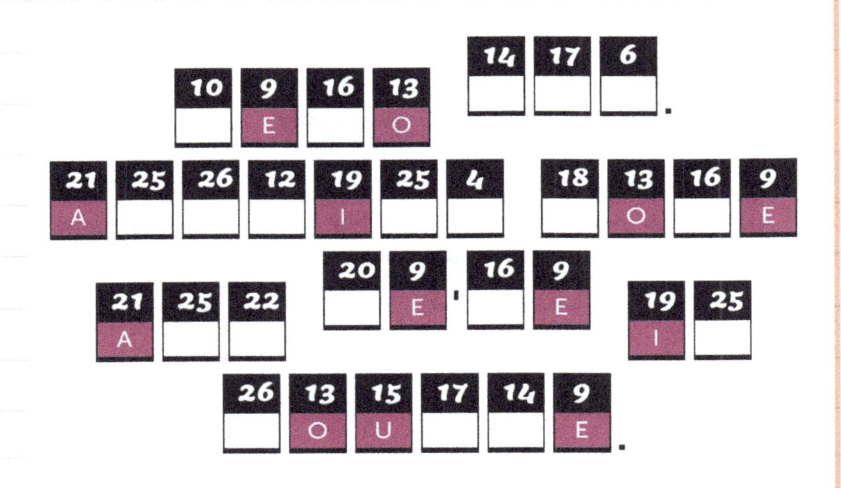

Answer on page: 213

Joke - 4

A man told fart jokes then one day just stop. Why do you think he stop telling fart jokes?

- Solve the Crytogram puzzle to finish the joke.

CRYPTOGRAM KEY:

ANSWER:

Answer on page: 213

Joke - 5

What would happen if you farted while traveling at the speed of sound?

ANSWER:

would the smell hit you before you heard it?

Joke - 6

Farting on an elevator is the worst. Why?

* Solve the Crytogram puzzle to finish the joke.

CRYPTOGRAM KEY:

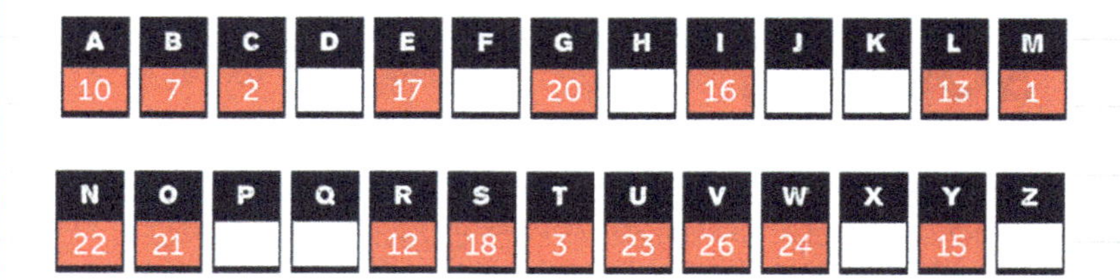

ANSWER:

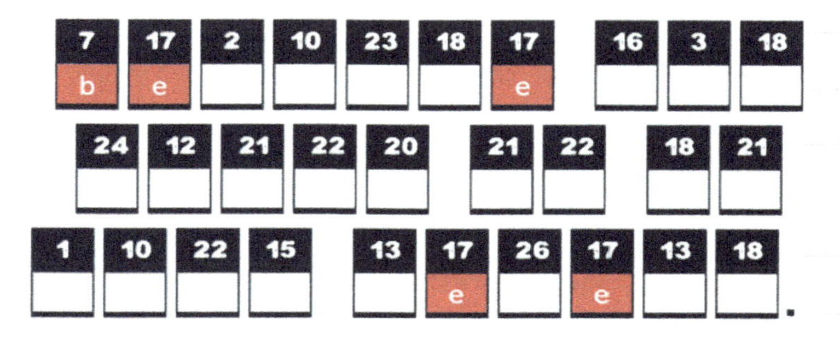

Answer on page: 213

Joke - 7

What do you call people who farts by themselves?

* Solve the Crytogram puzzle to finish the joke.

CRYPTOGRAM KEY:

A	B	C	D	E	F	G	H	I	J	K	L	M
17				25				20				

N	O	P	Q	R	S	T	U	V	W	X	Y	Z
	14	11		13		21		9				

ANSWER:

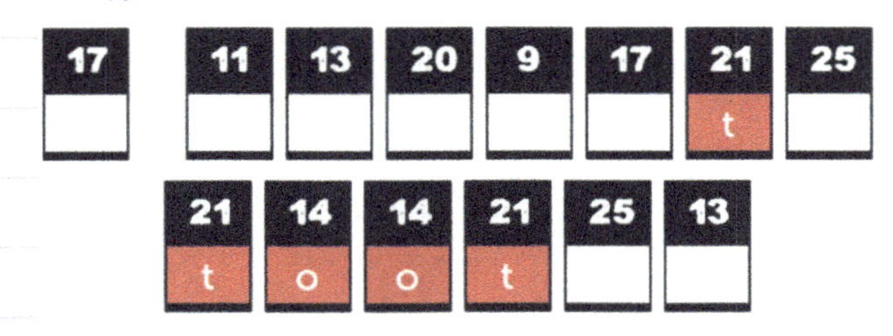

17		11	13	20	9	17	21	25
							t	

21	14	14	21	25	13
t	o	o	t		

Answer on page: 213

Joke - 8

Why would someone fart on their wallet?

ANSWER:

To get gas money

Joke - 9

Who put Dumpty back together again?

* Solve the Crytogram puzzle to finish the joke.

CRYPTOGRAM KEY:

A	B	C	D	E	F	G	H	I	J	K	L	M
	7	8	2		6	21	23		12	16	1	26

N	O	P	Q	R	S	T	U	V	W	X	Y	Z
13		3	4	15	10	9		24	22	11	18	5

ANSWER:

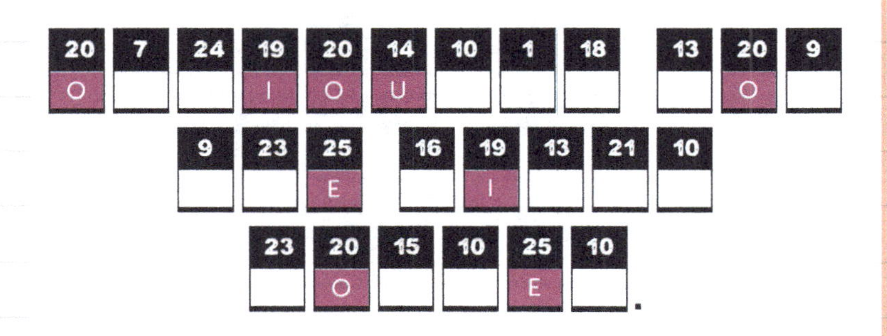

Answer on page: 209

Joke - 10

What really scared miss muphet off her tuffet?

* Solve the Crytogram puzzle to finish the joke.

CRYPTOGRAM KEY:

A	B	C	D	E	F	G	H	I	J	K	L	M
	4	14	22		24	6	12		10	25	16	2

N	O	P	Q	R	S	T	U	V	W	X	Y	Z
21		11	26	15	7	8		20	19	23	3	1

ANSWER:

Answer on page: 209

Joke - 11

What did Jack and Jill see when they went up the hill?

* Solve the Crytogram puzzle to finish the joke.

CRYPTOGRAM KEY:

A	B	C	D	E	F	G	H	I	J	K	L	M
	20	22	2		18	8	6		1	5	16	26

N	O	P	Q	R	S	T	U	V	W	X	Y	Z
9		10	14	4	21	24		17	25	13	19	23

ANSWER:

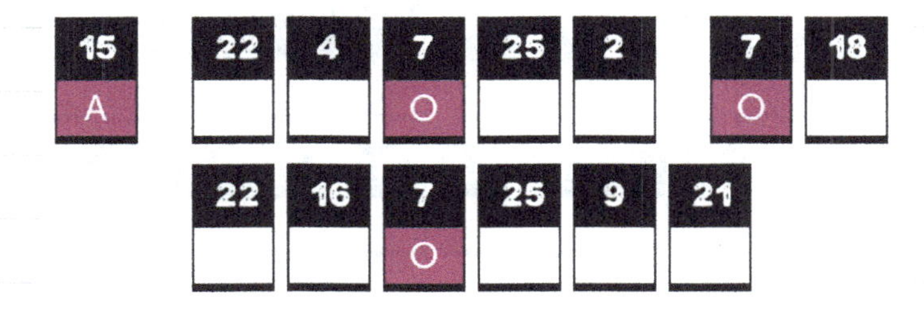

Answer on page: 209

Joke - 12

What did the spider say after miss muphet ran away?

* Solve the Crytogram puzzle to finish the joke.

CRYPTOGRAM KEY:

A	B	C	D	E	F	G	H	I	J	K	L	M
	22	10	1		11	19	20		23	6	9	16

N	O	P	Q	R	S	T	U	V	W	X	Y	Z
25		8	7	13	15	4		26	18	24	14	5

ANSWER:

Answer on page: 209

Joke - 13

What made Dumpty fall?

* Solve the Crytogram puzzle to finish the joke.

CRYPTOGRAM KEY:

A	B	C	D	E	F	G	H	I	J	K	L	M
	1	6	13		7	19	15		26	11	14	20

N	O	P	Q	R	S	T	U	V	W	X	Y	Z
3		8	2	12	24	23		5	10	4	16	17

ANSWER:

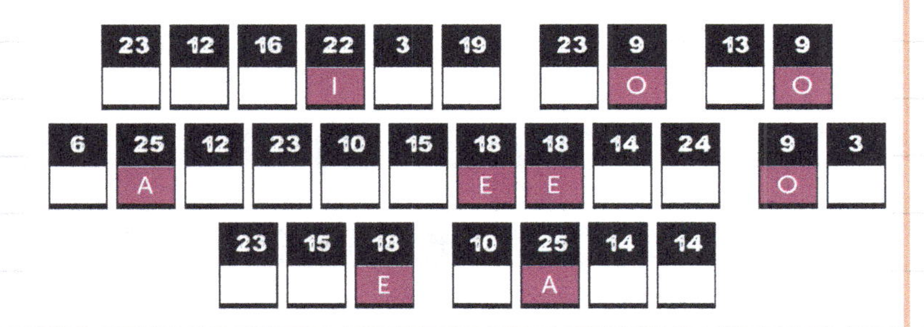

Answer on page: 209

Joke - 14

What made the bridge in London fall?

* Solve the Crytogram puzzle to finish the joke.

CRYPTOGRAM KEY:

A	B	C	D	E	F	G	H	I	J	K	L	M
	21	3	9		8	26	13		12	4	2	1

N	O	P	Q	R	S	T	U	V	W	X	Y	Z
20		15	19	24	10	18		7	14	23	25	11

ANSWER:

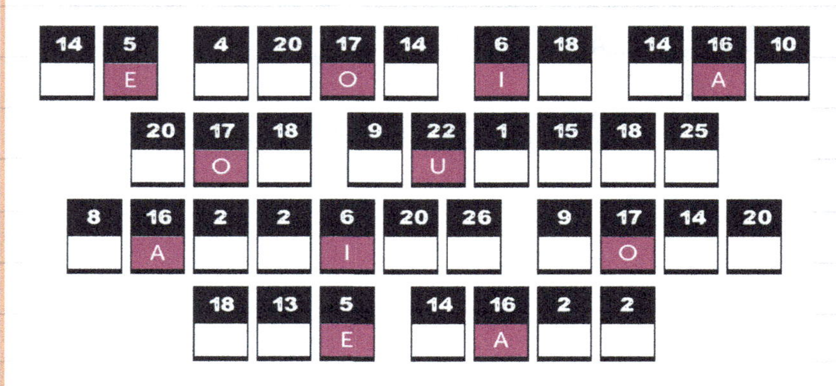

Answer on page: 209

Joke - 15

What did the left wall say to the right wall?

* Solve the Crytogram puzzle to finish the joke.

CRYPTOGRAM KEY:

A	B	C	D	E	F	G	H	I	J	K	L	M
	20	6	8		24	1	23		26	12	22	4

N	O	P	Q	R	S	T	U	V	W	X	Y	Z
7		11	19	15	18	13		3	14	21	17	2

ANSWER:

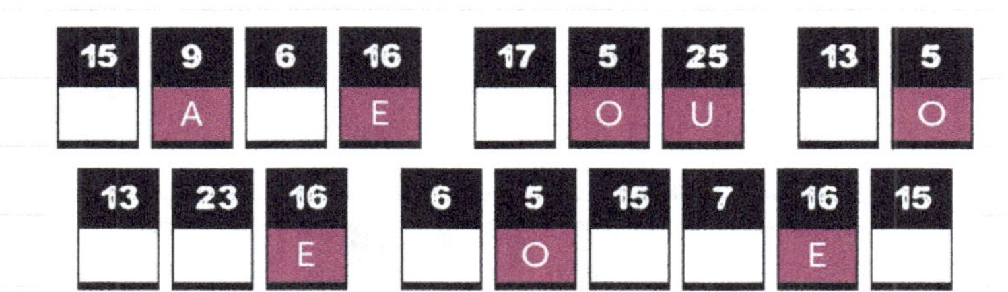

Answer on page: 209

Joke - 16

Why is the river richer than the sea and the ocean?

* Solve the Crytogram puzzle to finish the joke.

CRYPTOGRAM KEY:

A	B	C	D	E	F	G	H	I	J	K	L	M
	24	21	7		15	23	25		1	3	11	17

N	O	P	Q	R	S	T	U	V	W	X	Y	Z
2		12	14	13	19	5		4	9	22	10	18

ANSWER:

Answer on page: 209

Joke - 17

How do flags say hi?

* Solve the Crytogram puzzle to finish the joke.

CRYPTOGRAM KEY:

A	B	C	D	E	F	G	H	I	J	K	L	M
	17	14	11		6	7	9		16	22	12	26

N	O	P	Q	R	S	T	U	V	W	X	Y	Z
23		20	24	15	3	4		18	5	1	13	10

ANSWER:

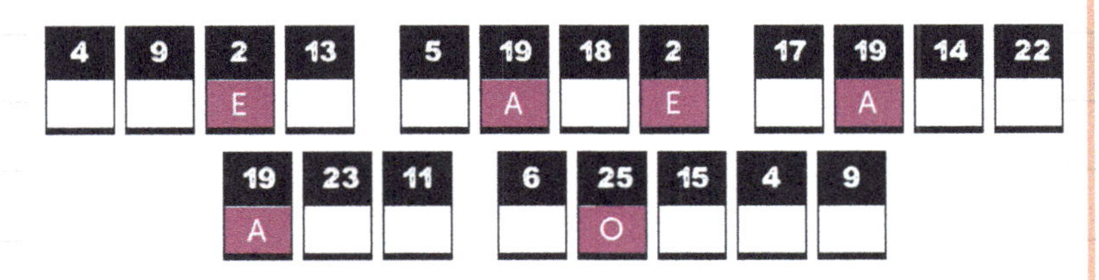

Answer on page: 209

ALGORITHM FUN

Real World connect:

Did you know? We use Algorithms every day.

* #1 - Brush your teeth,
* #2 - Clean your room
* #3 - Build that extra cool tree house that has space station controls.

You use Algorithms every day to follow steps to complete a task. Now you can have some fun following certain steps in the mazes to find out more about the S.D Agents!

The next few pages will have code instructions so that you can unlock clues about the S.D Agents.

KEY CODE

* The "number" will show how many spaces you are to move.
* The following symbols tell you the direction to move

R	Move Right
L	Move Left
U	Move Up
D	Move Down

Example: 5U (this means move up 5 spaces from where you are on the board, don't count the space you're in.)

All about AI

What do I like to do in my spare time?

2L,2D,1R	=	

What do I eat every chance I can?

1L,1D,3L,4D,2R	=	Lemons

What do I want for my birthday?

3D,2L,1D,3L,2D	=	

All about AI part 2

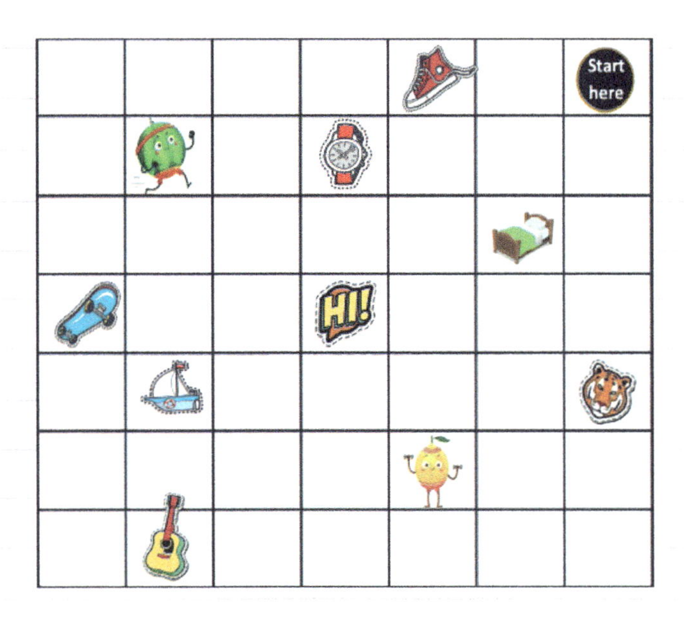

What does my sister like to eat?

2D,5L,1U	=	

What's my favorite ice cream flavor?

1D,3L,4D,1R	=	

What do I like to do everyday?.

2L,2D,1R	=	

All about Allie

What do I like to do in my spare time?

1L, 4D, 1L, 1D, 3L	=	

What's my favorite ice cream flavor?

4L, 1D, 2R	=	

I don't like this food.

4L, 4D, 3R	=	

All about Allie part 2

Start here

What do I eat when I watch movies?

3L, 2D, 3R	=	

What do I want for Christmas?

4D, 3L, 2D	=	

What did my sister give me for my birthday?

2D,4L,2U,1L	=	

All about Dee

What do I like to do in my spare time?

2R, 4D, 2R, 1U, 1R	=	

What's the best gift I've ever gotten?

6R, 6D, 3L, 3U, 2R	=	

What's my favorite thing to do when I'm alone?

1D, 4R, 2D, 2L, 3D	=	

The Details on Dee

Start here						
			HI!			

What did I give my brother as a gift?

2D, 2R, 2U, 1R	=	

I love to watch this

3D, 2R, 2U, 3R	=	

What do I have on my bedroom wall?

4R, 3D, 1R, 2D	=	

All about Patty

What do I like to do in my spare time?

4D, 3R, 1D	=	

What's the best gift I've ever gotten?

2R, 2D, 3R, 1D	=	

What do I want for my birthday?

6R, 6D, 5L	=	

The Particulars of Patty

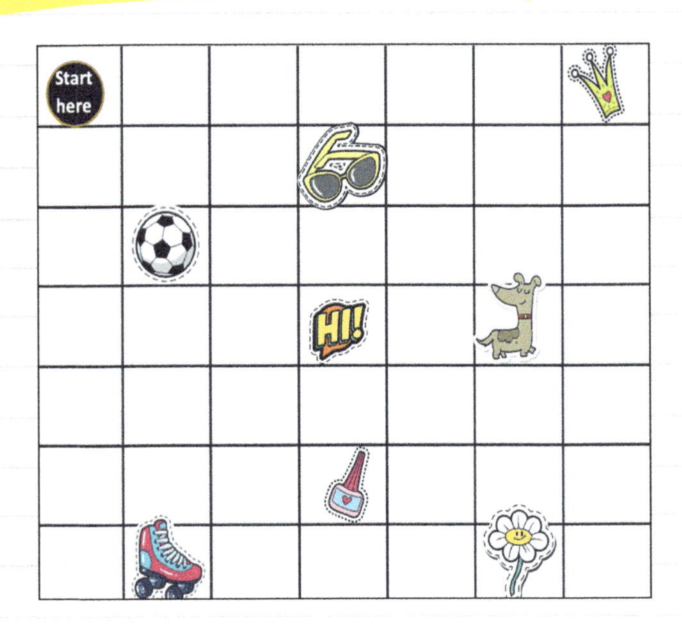

What was in my yard as a gift?

2D, 5R, 1D	=	

What did I get my bestfriend for her birthday?

2D,2R,1U,1R	=	

What makes me happy?

4D,3R,2D,2R	=	

All about Mac

What do I like to do in my spare time?

2R, 2D, 3R	=	

What's the best gift I've ever gotten?

6R, 4D, 1L	=	

Would I rather live in a world made entirely from Legos?

4D, 2R, 5U	=	

Random Facts about Mac

		YES!				
Start here						WHY?
			HI!			
	NO!					

Did I break Dee's mom's favorite dish?

3D,1R,1D	=	

Am I going to a water park this summer?

5D,2R,6U	=	

What did my aunt give me for Christmas last year?

1D, 4R,2U	=	

All about ____________

We couldn't leave you out. Tell us about you.

If you could choose one fantastic animal to have as a pet, what would you choose? And why?

If you could live like any bug, which would you trade places with? and why?

If you were a robot, what would your main function be? Why would that be your main function?

If you were a famous hero, what would you be famous for doing?

If you ran a toy company, what would be your next great toy to sell?

Mini mysteries #1 - Guess who?

INSTRUCTIONS:

Begin counting at the "Start Here" square and use the code from each question on the next page to solve the mystery.

Remember the number is the amount of spaces you move and the letter is the direction

* Example - "2R" means "move 2 spaces to the right."
* R = Right, L = Left, D = Down and U = Up

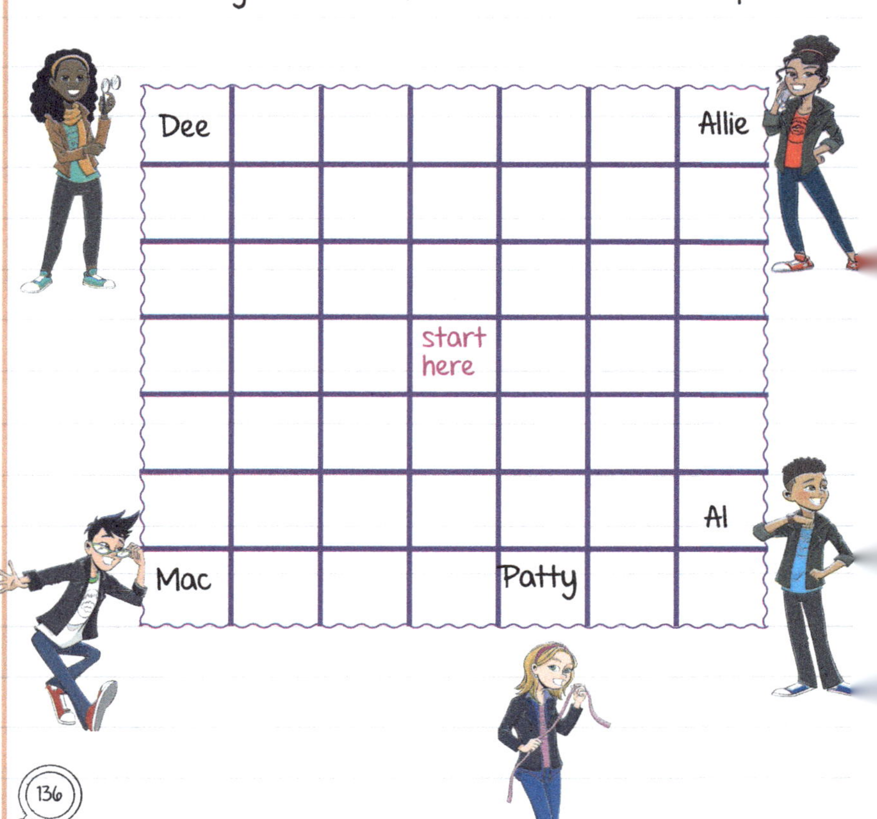

#1 I bet you'd never guess, who eats the fastest....

Use the code below to find out who??:

#2 OOOOOoooo who broke Dee's mom's favorite dish???

Use the below code to find who did it.

2R,2D,1R	=	

#3 This detective has 5 brothers and sisters.

Use the code below to find out who??

Answer on page: 208

Mini mysteries #2 - Guess who?

INSTRUCTIONS:

Begin counting at the "Start Here" square and use the code from each question to solve the mystery.

Remember the number is the amount of spaces you move and the letter is the direction

* Example - "2R" means "move 2 spaces to the right."
* R = Right, L = Left, D = Down and U = Up

Dee						Allie
			start here			
						Al
Mac				Patty		

#1 **Someone got a new dog this week and he ate all of Allie's chips.**

Use the code below to find out who??:

2L,3D,3R	=	

#2 **Guess who got an extra hour of recess because they figured out the puzzle first?**

Use the below code to find who did it:

2L,3U,1L	=	

#3 **This person designed her teacher's birthday outfit!**

Use the code below to find out who??

2D,2R,5U,1R	=	

Answer on page: 208

Mini mysteries #3 - Guess who?

INSTRUCTIONS:

Begin counting at the "Start Here" square and use the code from each question to solve the mystery.

Remember the number is the amount of spaces you move and the letter is the direction

* Example - "2R" means "move 2 spaces to the right."
* R = Right, L = Left, D = Down and U = Up

#1 This detective is an only child and will get a new dog soon.

Use the code below to find out who??:

#2 My favorite thing to do is riddles.

Use the below code to find who did it.

3R,1D,6L,2D	=	

#3 If I had a superpower, it would be to fly. I could go around the world in the blink of an eye.

Use the code below to find out who??

2R,2D,1R	=	

Answer on page: 208

Mini mysteries #4 - Guess who?

INSTRUCTIONS:

Begin counting at the "Start Here" square and use the code from each question to solve the mystery.

Remember the number is the amount of spaces you move and the letter is the direction

* Example - "2R" means "move 2 spaces to the right."
* R = Right, L = Left, D = Down and U = Up

Dee						Allie
			start here			
						Al
Mac				Patty		

#1 I like baseball and scored a homerun last week.

Use the code below to find out who??

#2 I love to write and to tell stories about all kinds of fun!

Use the below code to find who??

2L,2U,5R,1U =

#3 My nickname is doodle because I'm always drawing a new invention.

Use the code below to find out who??

2D,3L,5U =

Answer on page: 209

Mini mysteries #5 - Guess who?

INSTRUCTIONS:

Begin counting at the "Start Here" square and use the code from each question to solve the mystery.

Remember the number is the amount of spaces you move and the letter is the direction

* Example - "2R" means "move 2 spaces to the right."
* R = Right, L = Left, D = Down and U = Up

#1 Whose cat always finds it's way into the school yard?

Use the code below to find out who??:

#2 The last time we went camping, I saw a spi-der the size of my hand.

Use the below code to find who??

#3 I won a pancake eating tournament.

Use the code below to find out who??

3R,3D,2R =

Answer on page: 209

Training Completed!

You're OFFICIALLY a

Spy Detective (S.D) Agent!

HERE ARE YOUR WINGS!

GO TO PAGE 166 FOR MORE DETECTIVE FUN!

The Kid Code Mysteries!

Now that you've finished the training we have a urgent case we just started. We don't know all the details yet but we wanted to debrief you on the case.

A GRIMM DAY...

Hi... You ever had that odd feeling? It's sits right in the middle of your stomach like you ate sour milk or something? That's exactly how I feel. It seems like a normal Wednesday morning but by no means do our days end normally.

My name is Dee, and my friends Mac, Patty, Al and Allie go to Manchester Middle School by day but afterschool we're Spy Detectives. **This is my spy notebook, I don't want to miss a thing, so I write *everything* down and draw important details. Hence,** you'll be with me every step of the way today. Come on, let's get going, today is an important day...

I already did the typical stuff you do, like brushing your teeth and washing your face. Get this, I even flossed! So, I'm ready.

I have to run past my brothers' room or else I'll be knocked out! It always smells like a mix of onion rings, old cheese, and stinky farts lingering from last week.

Whew! I made it out of the house with my senses intact and even managed to grab some breakfast.

* * *

Walking into school I passed Julian right as his green gloves slammed into his locker. He wears green gloves with red fingertips everywhere. Even in the summer, his gloves never leave his fingers. I put a hand on his shoulder, "Hey, are you ok?"

"No," he grunted. I've been trying to put this combination in for 3 whole minutes! The lines are too small! Who makes lines that small? Ugh!"

Taking the gloves off would help quite a bit, I thought. My best friend Patty came along. "Trouble with the lock again?"

"Yeah, it sucks," he sneered.

"You mean it's stuck. Let me try." Patty started sliding the numbers to the combination so smoothly I thought I heard a violin playing in the background. The lock just popped open.

"You're good at this, Patty." We went down the hall to our lockers. "Why does he wear those gloves all the time?" I asked... then shrugged "Actually, it's cool, he's original... because there are way too many copies around here. Speaking of original, I got an idea for a new lock. I can't wait to get to Professor E.B's this afternoon."

You ever had a crummy day at school where nothing was going right, and it seemed like everything, and

everybody just made no sense? We have a lot of those days at Manchester, but that's another story...

Professor E.B's lab is where we go and have fun. He's really funny and kind of quirky. He's always positive, and just knows how to let a kid be a kid. He said he came from the Great Inventor's Organization (GIO). At GIO, he learned to invent amazing things to help people. But one day he decided to leave, and just showed up on our school's front lawn, and the rest was history.

He created the "The Code Agency" to take on cases from the neighborhood that the police need help solving. This is where we get to be Spy Detectives. Our special op's name is "S.D Agents". Just last week we found the secret to the pulsating nasty green meat from the cafeteria that was making everyone sick.

Our parents love Professor E.B too. Even though the last time they came to lab Patty's dad slipped on a whatchamathingy and skid into a hologram machine and almost got shot into the ceiling. Yeah, we make mistakes sometimes, but we never give up (we also keep the lab a lot cleaner now).

We're the cool geeks of the school. Well, not everyone thinks we're cool. But their opinions only matter if you make it matter. We don't let it matter.

Professor E.B always encourages us to work together and says we shouldn't be competitive with each other. He said not knowing that caused him a lot of heartache, but he never explains why. He always says,

"WE'RE BETTER TOGETHER THAN APART!"

It's hard to remember that sometimes, especially when someone thinks they're better than you. That's when he reminds us that everybody has unique qualities, and no one is better than anyone else.

Unique indeed - like our ability to scarf down pizza in .05443 seconds. On our last pizza excursion, Patty took a few sketches of our inventions, take a look.

Bzzz...

click

shoelace looper

For younger kids

The hugging chair

if you ever need a hug and no one is around

stairs turn into a slide

The stair slide

Shhh...

Dog-O-Muter

(it doesn t hurt the dog and their barks can t hurt your ears)

Well, some of our inventions are still trial and error, but Professor E.B's latest invention puts the icing on a double decker triple layer cake! Figure that one out!

* * *

The day was moving slower than a slug on a log. But finally, it was lunch time.

Patty and I stood in the lunch line and I looked up and saw him. Who? One of our school's fastest racers. He wasn't bad to look at either. His name was Noah.

"I know you're glad you don't have to race against Parker, Finley or Jackson." His friend nudged him, and he almost fell into me. Our eyes met and I promise I heard music somewhere.

"Sorry about that." He smiled at me, turned back to his friend, and returned the nudge. "Cut it out. I'm not worried about them. I let my running talk for me."

We finally made it to the front and what the lunch lady slapped on my tray looked better than the green meat, but it sure didn't smell better.

We found Mac, Al and Allie huddled around a sketch of Professor E.B's latest invention.

"What did you find out?" I plopped my tray on the table and sat down.

"Hey D2E and P2!" Mac nodded his head and grinned, then went back to the sketch. He loves brain teasers so much he sometimes talks to us in riddles.

Al and Allie were buried in their tablets, "We're trying to figure out what the code is doing. It changes every 5 minutes, kind of like my little brother's attitude." Allie said.

Al scrunched up his face "Yeah, I could say you change every 5 minutes too. You're only 3 minutes older than me, but I'm 3 centimeters taller, so not exactly 'little', as far as you're concerned. Get a clue, Shorty."

"I'm 3 minutes older than you, and 3 times smarter. You, get a clue, Big Foot." Allie smirked.

The twins Al and Allie were always making snide remarks at each other, but they're extremely smart. In fact, a year ago, our principal, Mr. Field, hired them to hack into the school's website to find out who posted um... pictures of one our teachers.

Back to Professor E.B's new invention. It's a machine that allows technology to morph into new shapes and sizes; it's called "Automorphism" code name "AMP." The AMP will help create new metal and equipment to give people new body parts, like hearts and legs. It can even create new airplanes that are safer.

Today is the day Professor E.B lets us test the controls to get the kinks out of it.

WE'RE ABOUT

PERCENT SURE IT'S GOING TO WORK.

We were hunched over the sketch when we saw green gloves with red fingertips cover half the picture. We looked up and saw Julian. I forgot to mention, he's a S.D informant. He talks when he wants to and *sometimes* knows the right information.

"Hey" he moved a piece of hair from his forehead. We looked up at him fully expecting him to give us something. We didn't know what that "something" was, but we knew it was something.

"I was walking to the lunchroom and I heard some loud shouting and banging coming from the lab."

All of a sudden, the cafeteria doors flung open and in ran Mr. Field, gasping for air. His belly proceeded him as he stopped to catch his breath.

"It's gone!"

Our eyes widened. What in the world was he talking about? I looked over at Mac and pushed his chin up to close his mouth.

"Professor E.B and the AMP! I went to look for him, the lab is a mess, and there is no sign of him. He's gone!" It was like a shockwave hit us and we couldn't move. What happened!?

"There's a message on one of his computers." He looked at us and waved for us to follow him. We sprinted down the hall so fast you would think we had on skates.

We ran into the science lab, around the bird cage, and hit a red button (Professor E.B created a sweet entry into his lab). We started down the stairs, the lights were on, but there was no sound or movement.

That's when things got really strange. When we got down to the lab, we saw it had been ransacked. All the papers and inventions were thrown on the floor.

"What happened here?" Mac stooped down and picked up the hand car washer and sat it on the table.

"I don't know, but we're going to get to the bottom of this." I went to the computer screen. It was open and blinking. It said Word scramble

"IGMRM SYAS OOKL NI EHT ILFE BACNIET."

Mr. Field looked at the computer "That's what I saw." As soon as he said those words, he started making weird bleeping and buzzing noises, and his head started bobbing up and down, side to side. His arm popped out, making Mac jump and I let out a shriek. As we all stood staring, we realized this wasn't Mr. Field at all! This was a......robot!

"Whoaa! What just happened?" Mac moved to the other side of the room.

"I have no idea. It's a robot, but it looks just like

Mr. Field, our principal." I cupped my mouth.

"Things just got realllllyyy weird." Al poked at the arm.

"Why would Mr. Field be a Robot?" Allie moved to take a closer look.

The robot principal jumped and started buzzing again like it was starting up and we all grabbed a weapon. Granted we only had a bat, two chairs, the hand car washer, and... I looked at Patty "What are you going to do with a stapler?"

"I'll staple his eye out, if I have to!"

The robot sparked again and when he opened his mouth, he sounded nothing like Mr. Field. But we knew that voice. It was GRIMM.

"Hello Kiddies! I see you've found the message I left you. Aren't I clever?" "When you solve the clue, you'll know what to do." HAHAHA. Sneeze. Wheeze. "This message will now self-destruct." The principal robot started to smoke and in a matter of seconds, just vanished before our eyes.

It was one of GRIMM's Cyborgs. What is he up to and how did he get a Cyborg to look just like our principal? "This is crazy," I said.

"Where is the real Mr. Field? Where is Professor E.B?" Patty put the stapler in her bookbag.

"He must have used Professor E. B's AMP to make his Cyborgs morph into people. We have to find Professor E.B and the AMP before GRIMM uploads the AMP into all of his Cyborgs." I gave everyone paper and a pen, "We need to figure this out."

It didn't take long before we worked out the message

"GRIMM SAYS LOOK IN THE FILE CABINET."

We all ran over to the file cabinet, opened the top drawer, and there it was. A note.

"I have your beloved professor and the AMP! There is nothing you can do about it. He thinks you're all smarter than I am, and if I leave you clues, you'll be able to figure it out and stop me! I think he's wrong, of course. I've always won against his students so you're no match for me. I left a case for you to solve. If you solve it, I'll contact you with the next case, and so forth. If you can't figure it out then it's cyber life for Professor E.B and he'll be controlled by me. Let's see if you can break "The Kid Code."

-GRIMM"

1 Help us solve the case!

We need all the help we can get to solve these cases. We need to get the AMP back and Professor E.B

Professor E.B told us that he and GRIMM worked closely together at GIO. They were the same age, but GRIMM came to GIO a few years later. You could say he was GRIMM's teacher. Professor E.B taught lots of people at the GIO lab. GRIMM was really smart, so he went through the classes quick and that's when the problems started. GRIMM would setup competitions between him and Professor E.B to see who was smarter, or who could solve puzzles quicker, or who could create the best inventions. He said they had a complicated friendship. It had to be complicated because from what he told us GRIMM lost most of the time. He could win against the other GIO lab students, but it was rare that he beat Professor E.B.

HE SAID THAT ONE DAY WHILE THEY WERE WORKING IN THE GIO LAB, GRIMM LOST HIS TEMPER AND SNAPPED. PROFESSOR E.B DIDN'T KNOW WHY, BUT GRIMM WAS AGITATED, YELLING, AND CAUSING LOTS OF ABRUPT LITTLE EXPLOSIONS EVERYWHERE. HE WAS ANGRY AND GOING A BIT CRAZY, AND THINGS STARTED TO CATCH FIRE. PROFESSOR E.B THOUGHT HE NEEDED TO DO SOMETHING QUICK, OR ELSE THE BUILDING WOULD CATCH ON FIRE. SO, HE HASTILY USED ONE OF HIS INVENTIONS TO STOP HIM. IT WAS AN ELECTRIC CYBORG THAT WAS IN THE PROCESS OF BEING BUILT; IT MALFUNCTIONED, AND THE ROBOTIC ARM SLAMMED INTO GRIMM'S RIGHT EYE.

Before anyone could get help, GRIMM ran away swearing revenge on Professor E.B. Now GRIMM creates Cyborgs on his own, but they aren't for helping people. He wants to use them for stealing and committing fiendish crimes. He plans to take over the world with his Cyborgs, and he thinks NO ONE can stop him. GRIMM was once a great inventor, but now has a circuit loose because he made a turn for the worse that day. Using Professor E. B's technology, he has another piece to complete his plan. His Cyborgs would be able to morph into everyday people we know. He must think because he beat Professor E. B's other students that it's easy to beat a bunch of middle schoolers. But he's more wrong than two left shoes.

As you can see his Cyborg was our principal, Mr. Field! Who knows, if we don't win at GRIMM's game, he might even try to take over the mayor of Manchester Falls.

We need to stop him and put an end to his deceiving ways. No one is safe with him on the loose. Remember, his Cyborgs could be anywhere, and morph into anyone or anything. Even your pet cat!

Help us unlock the codes in the cases so we can bring GRIMM to justice and put him where he belongs, behind bars. How can you help? I'm glad you asked. We take notes to solve crimes, but sometimes we miss things. When you finished the training you became a part of The Code Agency and as a member, you're now a S.D (Spy Detective) Agent.

What's next??

We will be in contact with you because we need your help to get Professor E.B back!!!

We can't do it without YOU! Be on the lookout for The GRIMM Kid Code...

Resources

1. *Help your kids with computer science: A unique visual step-by-step guide to computers, coding, and communication.* (2018). London: Dorling Kindersley Limited.
2. Chameleon. (2021, March 31). Retrieved April 09, 2021, from https://en.wikipedia.org/wiki/Chameleon
3. *Help your kids with computer coding: A unique step-by-step visual guide, from binary code to building games.* (2019). New York, NY: DK Publishing.
4. *The Teacher's Corner - Lesson Plans, Worksheets and Activities*, www.theteacherscorner.net/.

The GRIMM Kid Code

We'll need your help to beat GRIMM, get Professor E.B and the AMP back!

Unsolved Mysteries from Manchester Falls

There are a ton of mystery cases building up and we need your help to solve them.

Brain buzzing questions -
a good detective always takes notes. You can answer these questions or ask a friend or family member and take good notes.

Journal Entry 1

1What do you like daydreaming about?

Name:
Answer

What's a memory that makes you happy?

Name:
Answer:

Journal Entry 2

What do you look forward to when you wake up?

Name:
Answer

You're at the beach. What's the first thing you do?

Name:
Answer:

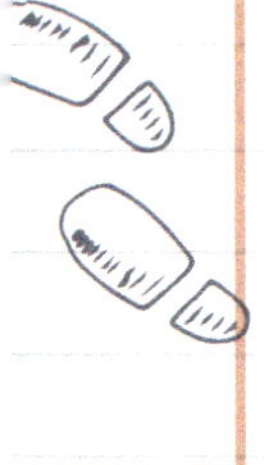

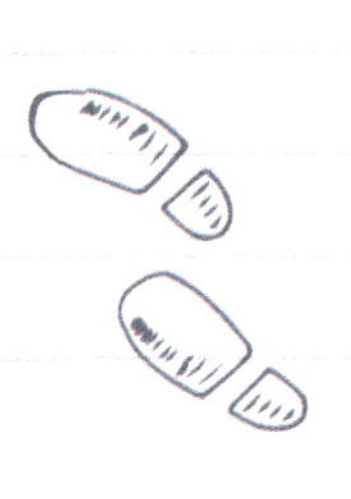

Journal Entry 3

What makes you feel brave?

Name:
Answer

What makes you feel loved?

Name:
Answer:

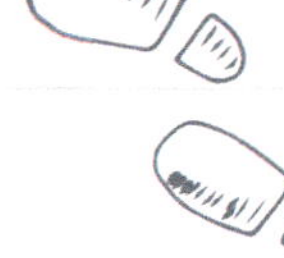

Journal Entry 4

How do you show people you care?

Name:

Answer

If you could give $100 to a charity, which would you choose? And Why?

Name:

Answer:

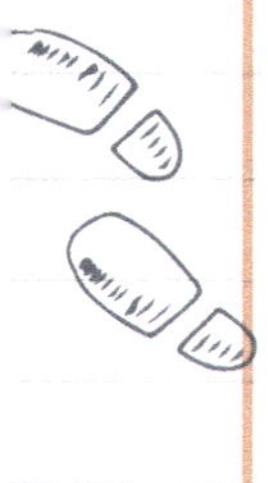
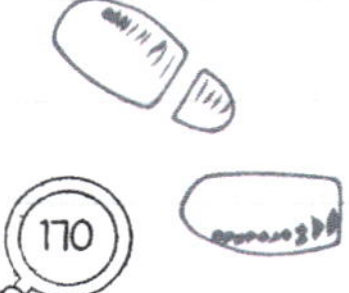

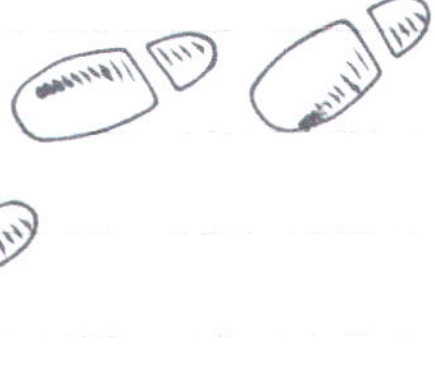
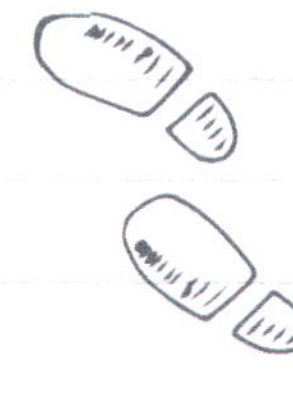

Journal Entry 5

How would you design a treehouse?

Name:
Answer

If you could design clothes, what would they look like?

Name:
Answer:

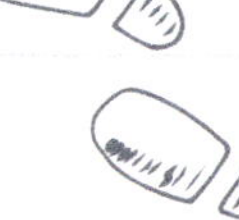

Journal Entry 6

How do you best like helping others?

Name:
Answer

What makes you feel thankful?

Name:
Answer:

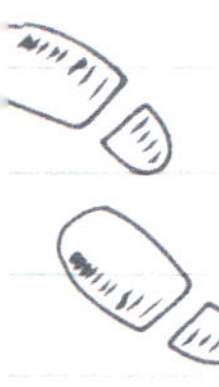

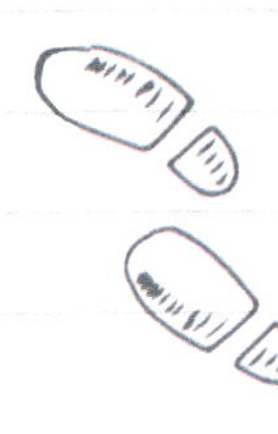

Journal Entry 7

If you made a cave in the woods, what would be inside it?

Name:
Answer

What makes you feel energized?

Name:
Answer:

Journal Entry 8

If you were in a play, what would your character be like?

Name:
Answer

What makes your friends so awesome?

Name:
Answer:

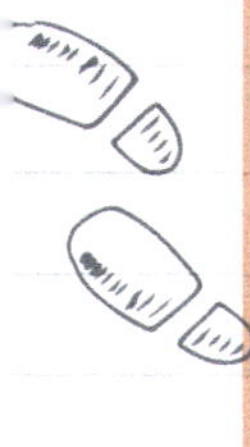
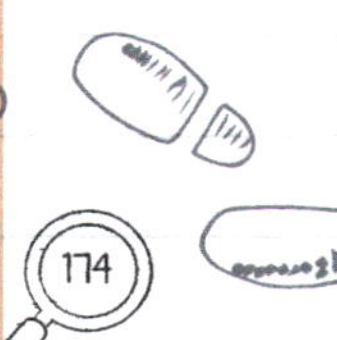
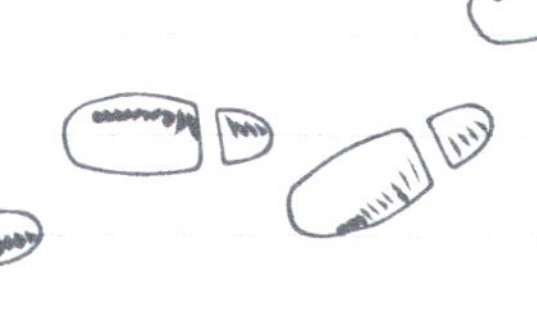
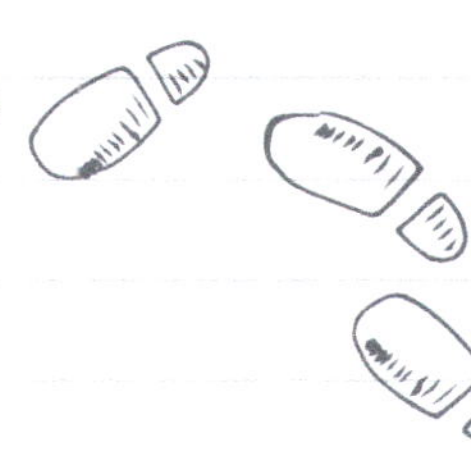

Journal Entry 9

What makes you so awesome?

Name:
Answer

What are three things you want to do this summer?

Name:
Answer:

Journal Entry 10

If you had friends all over the world, how would you keep in touch?

Name:
Answer

If you joined the circus, what would your circus act be?

Name:
Answer:

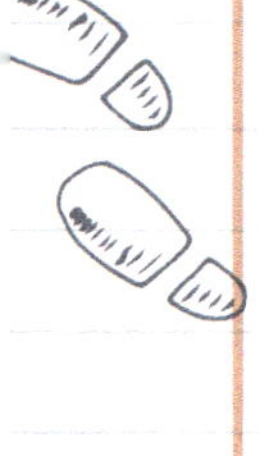

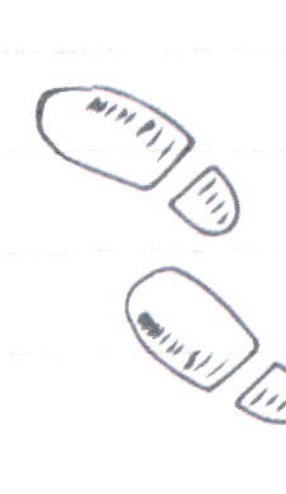

Journal Entry 11

If you were a teacher and could teach your students anything at all, what would you teach them?

Name:

Answer

If a friend asks you to keep a secret that you don't feel comfortable keeping, what would you do?

Name:

Answer:

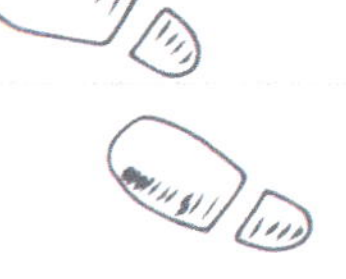

Here are some coloring pages with encouraging messages just for YOU!

Invent
IT

Dream
Big

Don't
give up

You're
Beautiful

You're
Smart

Be
the change
you
want to see.

No
Fear,
only
faith

The
world
needs
you

You
are
fearless

You
are
wonderful

Fear
Not

Hope
always

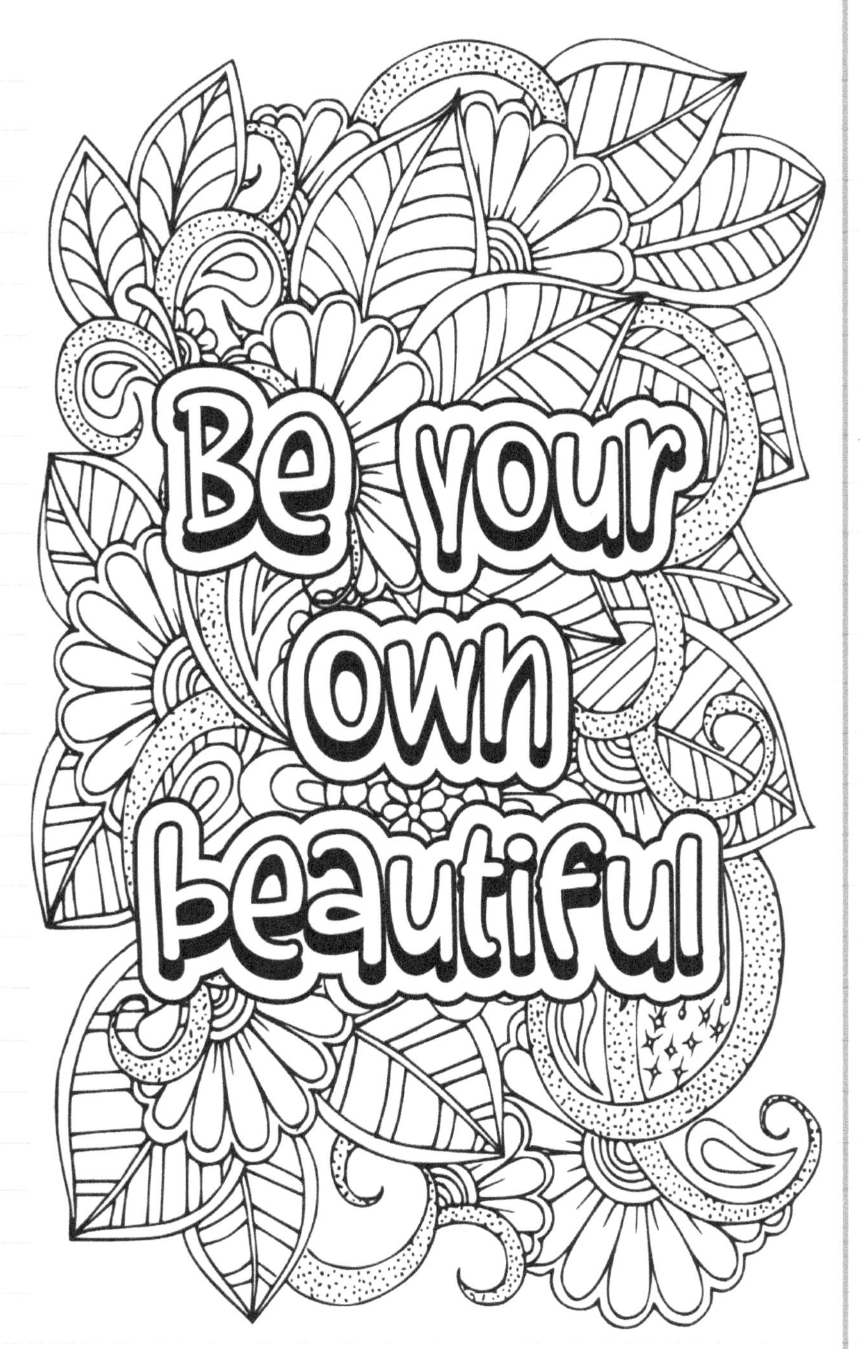
Be your
own
beautiful

Have
Fun

Smile.
Laugh.
Love

x = abc

The next few pages you're about to read are CLASSIFIED training that we give EVERY Spy Detective Agent.

"The Detective Code"

We use Computer Science and the inventions we create to solve our mysteries.

THE DETECTIVE CODE

S.D AGENTS ONLY

Definition

Examination allows you to study a problem so that you can dissect or separate the problem into smaller pieces. When you solve each of the smaller pieces you are closer to solving the original problem.

Computer connect

Computer Scientists use a similar process when writing a Computer program; it is called Modular Code. Modular Code is when a Computer Scientist takes a big problem and breaks it down into smaller problems, then writes a Computer program to solve each of the smaller problems.

"The Detective Code" Note

Imagine you have a case, and you walk into a room where a bubble gum machine just EXPLODED! Your mission is to unglue the mess and find the person who made the machine go POP. Would you dive headfirst into the bubble gum? No, that would have you glued to a sticky situation. You first must look for clues to find out who did it.

Definition

Abstraction is where you look at a problem and get rid of all the unnecessary information. After you have broken the problem down into smaller pieces, you need to find the key clues that will help you solve the problem (filter out unnecessary information).

Computer connect

A model is a way to represent a problem, or thing. Computer Scientists sometimes create test models of a computer program to see how it will work without wasting time on a solution that may not solve the problem. For example, if you wanted to represent a bridge with building blocks, the bridge you create would be called a "Model" of a bridge. To build the bridge, you would need to know the key parts of a bridge.

"The Detective Code" Note

In each of the cases, you must find the clues that matter. Each case will have codes that you need to break to find the keys to solve the case. For example, in the bubble gum case, the suspect plays the piano. If this clue has nothing to do with the case, then it's a clue that doesn't matter.

Patterns=

Definition

Patterns are all around us, and they help us in our daily lives. A pattern is something that is repeated multiple times and lets anyone who recognizes the pattern come to a conclusion.

Computer connect

We work smart not hard!

Computer Scientists look at patterns within computer code. If a new problem matches the pattern of an old problem, the Computer Scientist may reuse the code that fixed the old problem to solve the new problem.

"The Detective Code" Note

Back to the bubble gum case, if there is a clue that a girl called Emma always chews bubble gum and, in the story, it says the person left gum at the crime scene. You might think Emma is the thief. After all, she matches the clue (pattern) because she always chews bubble gum, and the thief left bubble gum at the crime scene.

Now we're going to talk about ALGORITHMS!

Definition

What are algorithms? A basic algorithm is a set of instructions or a list of steps to complete a task.

Computer connect

Computer programmers call algorithms "Computer code." Computer code is a set of instructions that tell the computer what to do, just like reading instructions on how to play your favorite game.

"The Detective Code" Note

In the cases, you will have the creative freedom to write instructions on what the Cyborg did to commit the crime. The correct answer will be in the answer section. In the bubble gum case, you have creative freedom to say how you suspect the person made the machine go pop!

Word puzzles:

1.

T R I I B O F N X L G A D Y P P A H L J
O I H X I Y U K M I Q H X I Q S O G R Y
W A J V X G N I R A D O D S M Y U E E P
Y K B F M G U W V S T S E N O H L N Q Z
L C V Y J D N I P I P J P G E D U U M G
I B V O Y O J L M G T K O O L Y F I F H
N D G O F J Q D C I T E G R E N E N A S
U Z K G R N B D K J G E I G R A P E B E
F V Y F I N V E L I R I Y E A M O V U B
C W I U E Y B T P Z A H N O E I H O L V
K E P N N M H E T R C Q F U X C M B O J
Y O N N D U R R R N I S A S C T G I U V
Z L J Y L A Z M K H O K U U I J V J S S
Q O G A Y U G I A Z U F N J T M Q S J A
K X K A L B O N E C S U O R E N E G R H
E V A R Q N Y E K G A E E W D E W P O N
P F O N U X X D K Q K G G R A T E F U L
F C A F C E X T R A O R D I N A R Y C X
C X H X A K O H Q N M U S W L L D T N J
N J Z A R C E F E A R L E S S C Y V J Q

2.

R W J Y P T E U Q N V B R Y F G V W R N
O O H V R N V O J U E E A J N N W F V T
P R E X N U E C V L O Y A L Q O Y Y Z S
T R Z F C E L B A V O L D R B R Y H E G
I R L U F T H G I S N I P R D T N W P G
M V P H N X V Y I E T V A W R S R T Z P
I N T E L L I G E N T D S H H D D W K V
S U T D M U S I C A L A S C G K I V M Y
T H N S C C Y N X M T L I J U H I S A F
I C D M H V C D Z U V A O J W D P U E K
C B N U D V N E Q H Z T N B G I O O L R
S B I S T S E P A Q H S A X Q B F E B G
V B K P A T G E L I Y P T N F T Y N I S
L O I Y F Y A N F X U P E A O G H A D I
W I D B Q E Z D G C N U R R V B Y T E K
J A R E D E T E C T I V E D K R M N R R
L N P W B V F N K E A O Q J A L J O C E
R Y T N X B I T P F L O V I N G S P N K
K V A G V A G M U X D H N B A K L S I F
F O Z F C T T U J O Y F U L O V E D H P

3.

U A V I M O N J N Y T Y T Z S T N P N F
X L A V H G S U K O G N I R A C U W P V
P C I D S H E C O U R A G E O U S H G F
E Z Q X F T H Z G R J V X G B C O V Y H
Q D A D V E N T U R O U S E N R H M M D
I U A M A Z I N G I T B R D D E N C D K
W L K V W M M N Z K A D Q T G A I E R N
X W E T A R E D I S N O C M C T F O J C
T Q D P K H A M G W I M N S I I Q O Z J
P W P U J N X U T L T H T V G V F I R B
E Z G H M F C V D D H K P Z Z E P U P T
D E T A N O I S S A P M O C S P L D Z U
X P C Z O H N K V C G S B P U B Z H Q O
E V A R B X A J Q F K O Q D O Y E X X S
D I F V Z I S D M W F L H O I F R Q N R
I P O O B G L H M K R A Q H T Z U E Q W
X D F G X J Q S Q Y N M X R I G W E Q Y
V X J N W M W B W Z K I A U B L R U C R
N F Q N N Z A U V V T W A L M D K H Y B
Y U L A T G X P Q D I H T U A N L S L S

4.

I O L O V E D X M B N J F K I G N U L A
N S C D U X L I O E Q Y P Q G Z Z T I O
D H N M Z J R I N C R E D I B L E M P C
E G T T X R G E F P J Q E N T T I A L L
P Z E J O G N I V O L P O S I T I V E E
E I Y R E U I S V M C N F I E F X R B F
N R R X U B R J M V I A H G E F Z S T T
D S U E O A I O U U C Y C H W P D X F U
E N F A I W P I E G X V Y T O X P D I S
N L D R N Y S Z R F Z I Q F J M Z S Y K
T O G D U O N T J A W X W U G W Q Z P H
H P T N E G I L L E T N I L N H I G J G
Y T D N I K L O Y A L U L N O C O X H K
I I A O O R L L E N B E Y F N S M T A Y
J M I G A J T U Y P A S S I O N A T E V
B I Y N S R V F K U L A C I S U M C F Y
G S F O R M H Y D Z E E L B A V O L P N
O T W R R S P O N T A N E O U S S A O Q
F I X T G N N J L B S X J W O N A W C M
I C S S R K P W U W E O C P J H P L C Y

5.

R C D D T L S W B Y M N O S T A W L M Q
O M J O D R N W R O Y N O Q E B V R W U
S A Y L L F Y B M N J C D K S A C W Y W
B K E K C O L R E H S I L C B M R I P H
D E T E C T G E G N Y Y M A W X W Q Z N
F R K F N S M P A U F J R V C O I Y C K
V M I Z X X J O D J I E B A C D Y J N G
A K F S T V H C V L N P Q W C S X R B C
G K D K M G U S W F G O F T C M J V P N
T P A M P L N E L J A C B Q I P K Q A U
N V L T S A K L W Z M S Y U X C Z U P H
E F G O A S Y E F N M O G C C F F F E R
G X O N L S V T M J R R H K A N E E R E
I Y R V J J O S R G E C U D E D U U N T
L Z I M S B D O N F J I P G R R K M D U
L A T Y K M T I H L E M T J A H E I N P
E O H B R A I N I A C M K L Z V S Q U M
T S M Q C K H H F I N G E R P R I N T O
N Q P E T C E F R E P C U I U I N D W C
I S N L D E D L N V E L D G P D K L V S

6.

B K Z X H X W G B Q B G D O E I W Y U C
U H D M E G A R U O C N E X N V N W X T
D D Q J K X Q O N P J R H V O S L F C W
M M L G T G M R F I R I I F N E Q C V C
W P H Y N I E Y D Z L G Z M Q I H M V C
D W S M T T J F T A O U H N X Q E I K R
W V L O N O H V R R Q L W O F P N N D P
L Q C Z L L O A A V Q H L L M J D S P W
U K P Y C R T T E N I M A X E I U W B G
V T J P B E E M U B D K Y X U I U H R I
Y D B A E Q T C M T W D P W K D R E S B
Q D Y T L K N E O G X L Y W O B V P W D
X Z J F S V U M T N X H Z E F O S F X S
P W S S J V A E N O N O K M C L P S T S
I I W F E G V T E Q T O Y S K U D J M D
S J G Z F U X A U Y C M I Q T N W H T L
X F V N M M S I T E B D I T A C I C D U
I J J W K O T W Q G H Z K L E T T Z N R
S L D A V P G U G U O C R D M R T E X T
D Z D Q O V E J V W Q X R E T K Y D N F

7.

E H W D J V M I K Y W F Z F S R Z I K D
E V W F A S U T C P W R M B X S I R D E
A Q C W G O F Z S C X W W E W X G C B L
A J H Y T L Y G H P E U V X L R O B F R
S X O T R G R B Q G D H E M U T L O C B
P P S T T P E L Z J S F I R N T N G R U
B M P K O Q A C H I E V E S V G R O H C
H Q O J X O A N L O K B C K X H U Z X T
R F E L A Y C P W A L H V H M I R N E S
O G X V B M M A N J Q B D I Z H F G X H
M Q X R S O E T B Y S C F Q C Q P C P S
S Y C I C U O T T M I K H Q D T I M E Y
D W J C D U K E G X N G I S E D C L Q H
D L A J B K I R G F E Y A E E R P B R W
U I O G D I E N Y C Q R R U E V T M Y H
O U Y F E P P F O A F I W B R V H Z H X
I I I R O T P E B L U E P R I N T Y K Z
P T Y Q P T Z Z N Q X O E Q T H R O L T
S O C D C D N A C Z X M G X G M N T K Q
O R H V M F B A P V P K Z L E W K H N E

8.

D R M B Q T W W I F Y D B Y G T H Z L U
B M Q A E I S C O K W L V M U B N F U D
D O B G S Z S Y X I W T Q W W Z O E F N
D T P Y I H W V E T D V K N D W J V R J
T E G A A U G G Z T U F C T N I S E E R
K C Y O R R A K I P A A H C M P Y V E G
V Z Y O S E U Y P K H V E R Q H O G H Q
T V W Y J D R N Y Y V D I J J R R W C P
C S C L B R U R J L N I Q T P O E I D R
F A S I H O E E K K V M F M L Q S T A X
W S F G R E S V U H G Q I W K U M L F Y
E W J H S U T O O A A G Y I P V C E E Z
B F Y N X J O C W G N M C S M Q D K T E
S S F A M M L W K A P Q E G B F P C A A
Y R X W Z V K Q T H W N M B Y Y K H E K
B N S I T C I V I I X Z R Z B T O W R R
K Z X C J M R N Q F F D C X T Y W I C E
S D N I B E Z C R K B F O N B Z V V G T
Z Q F T J Y R V O M G E A J H F Z P W P
P Q S L Z H M D Z O N A Y X K D E Z Q K

9.

U R R K Y B X M I I P Y G L U R M V S A
O X H V B H D Y H G E Y X E B X O S U M
N O H Q S K Z O J N J A H W H N F N O L
G G J Y K Q I M R I Y K P Z R S F X R G
Y N J C A P J V V M J M B M X Y N K O O
S N K X V R Z V D A X B K H M W V Q D G
K I S Q K M L A D E E M J W X U M L N S
M S S F Y J Z F Y L Z Z D G S A O I E A
W X J Q S Z Z X B G K R I M E V N T L I
T N Z A L H Q A Z J P M F A B N A O P I
C B F I K C R P L J W V W T I R S W S N
P R N S I O D R O D G G B H B A I U U D
R G B R M F D N L L Z V S E B H B G T O
O F I E F B V X W L U T L N H N G Z H G
H N M V E F A Z I V B E R C T V H T X T
L D T A U E J A T W C I S X L Z A P S R
S Y E X J R E W F C R P E P H A H U Y S
J E W C S N Z F M M M H A B I L Z T Y R
H J O V G K H V R A C K J V S B F M L A
F H B C Y B B B N Q M W L D J W A J C Z

10.

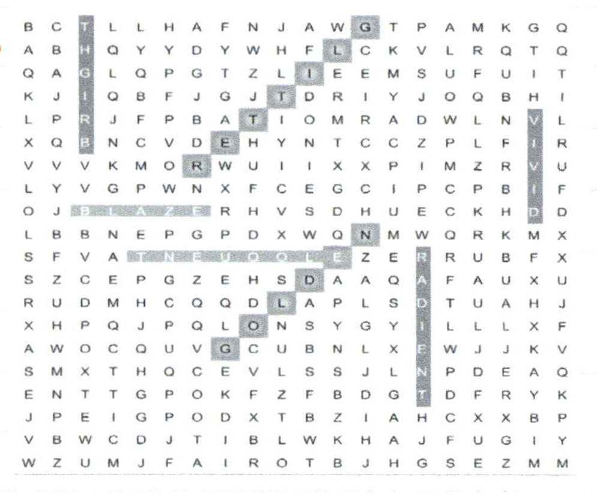

Rebus puzzles:

1. BIG BIRD
2. A CUT above the rest.
3. Blanket
4. Cross Bow
5. Get over it
6. Go for it

Riddle Answer:

Lettuce tell you something, treat us better or we'll make like a banana and split.

Mini Mystery 1:

1. Patty
2. Al
3. Allie

Mini Mystery 2:

1. Patty
2. Dee
3. Allie

Mini Mystery 3:

1. Mac
2. Mac
3. Al

Mini Mystery 4:

1. Al
2. Allie
3. Dee

Mini Mystery 5:

1. Al
2. Patty
3. Patty

Joke Answers:

8. To get gas money.
9. Obviously not the kings horses.
10. No one knows she is still running.
11. A crown of clowns.
12. See you again another day.
13. Trying to do cartwheels on the wall.
14. We know it was not Dumpty falling down the wall.
15. Race you to the corner.
16. Because of the riverbank.
17. They wave back and forth.

Maze:

1.

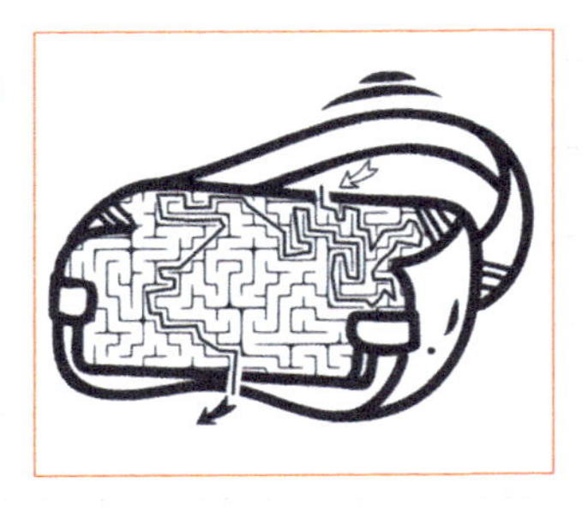

2.

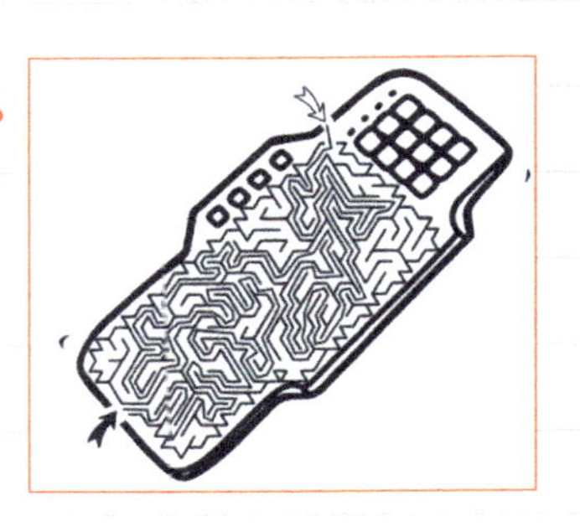

3.

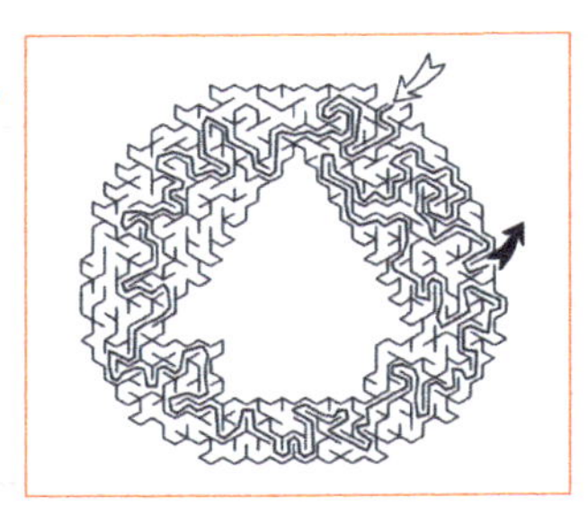

4.

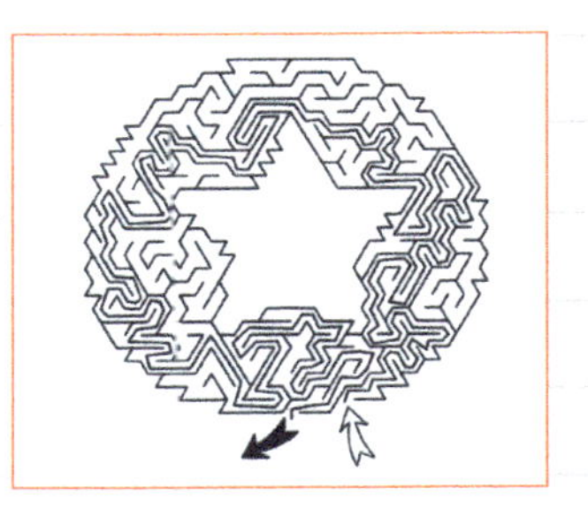

5.

6.

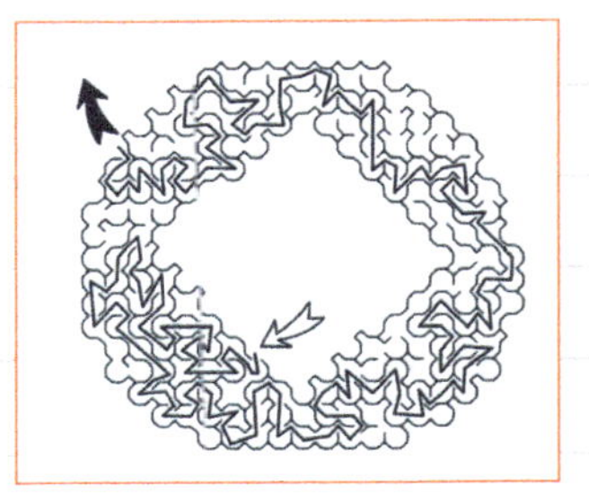

7.

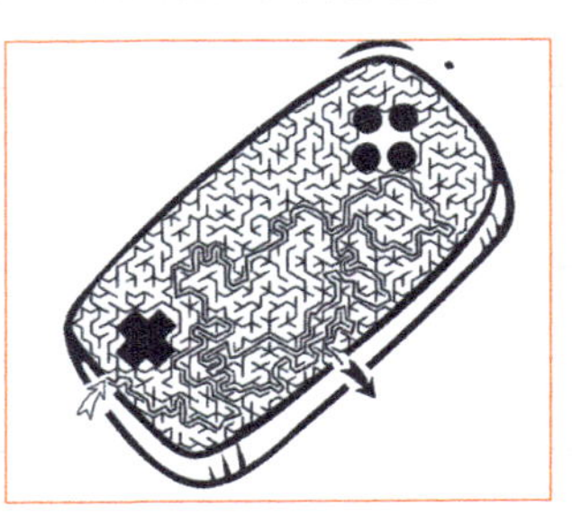

8.

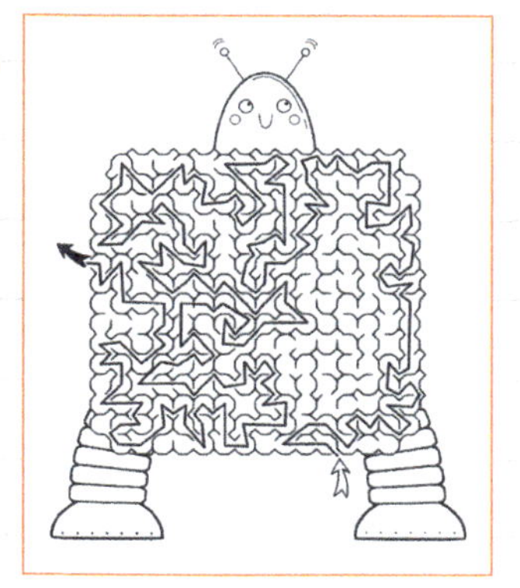

9.

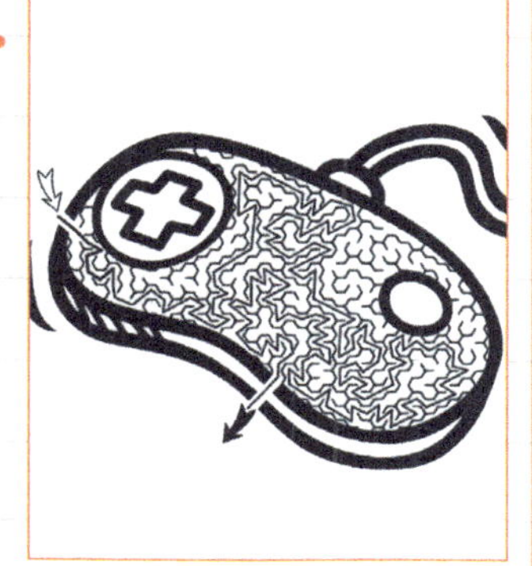

10.

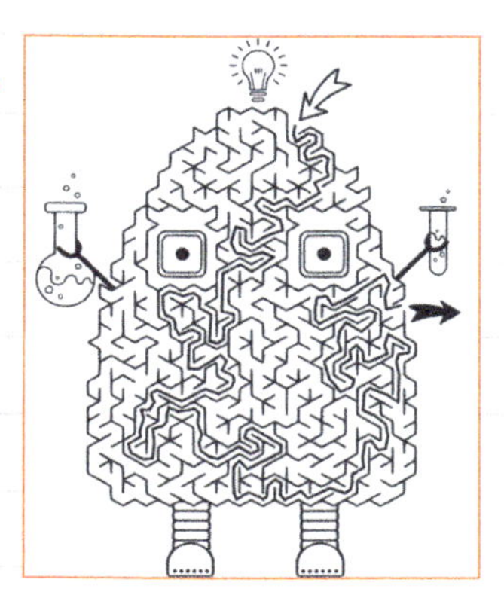

11.

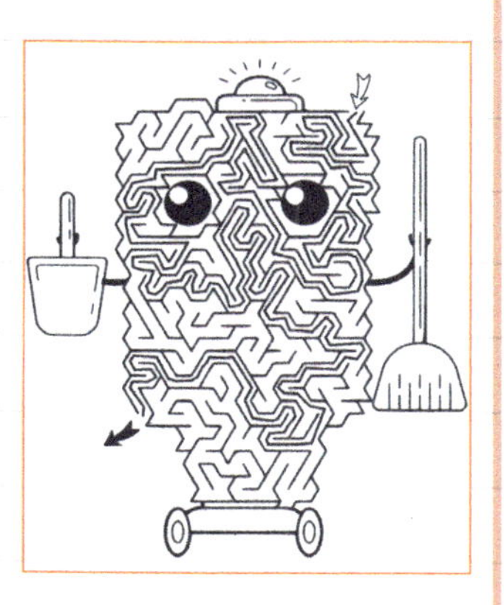

12.

13.

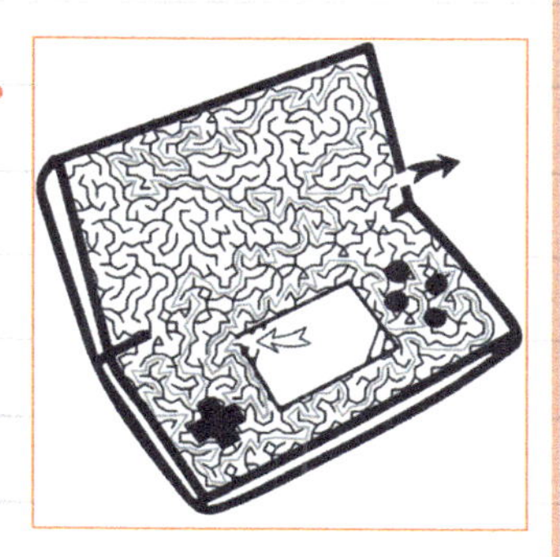

14.

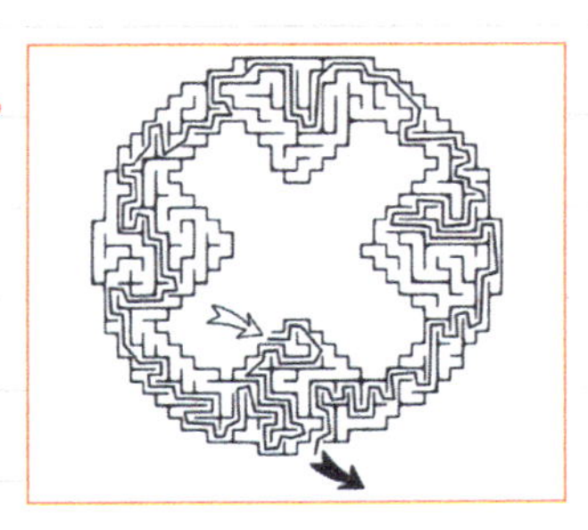

15.

16.

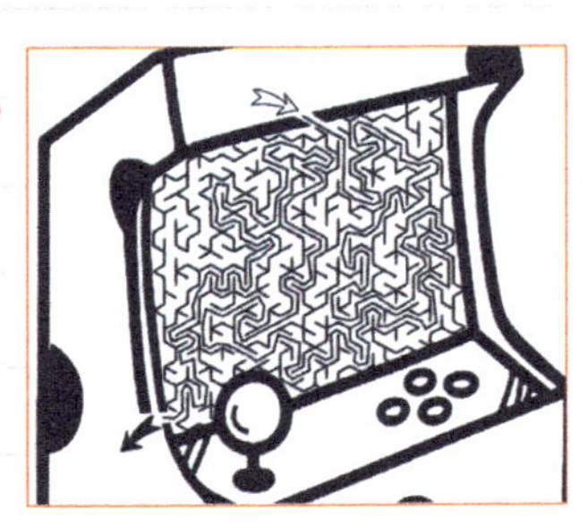

17.

18.

19.

20.

Joke Answers:

1. *Because I was totally blown away.*
2. *Think how many farts a couch has to endure in silence.*
3. *Zero lbs. Anthing more and we're in trouble.*
4. *Because his jokes stinks!*

Rebus puzzles:

7. Ice Cube
8. One in a Million
9. Sitting on top of the world
10. Time after time
11. Tuesday
12. Whose in Charge

Joke Answers:

5. *Would the smell hit you before you heard it?*
6. *Because it's wrong on so many levels.*
7. *A private tooter.*

Made in the USA
Coppell, TX
07 October 2023

22513780R10118